THE KABBALAH

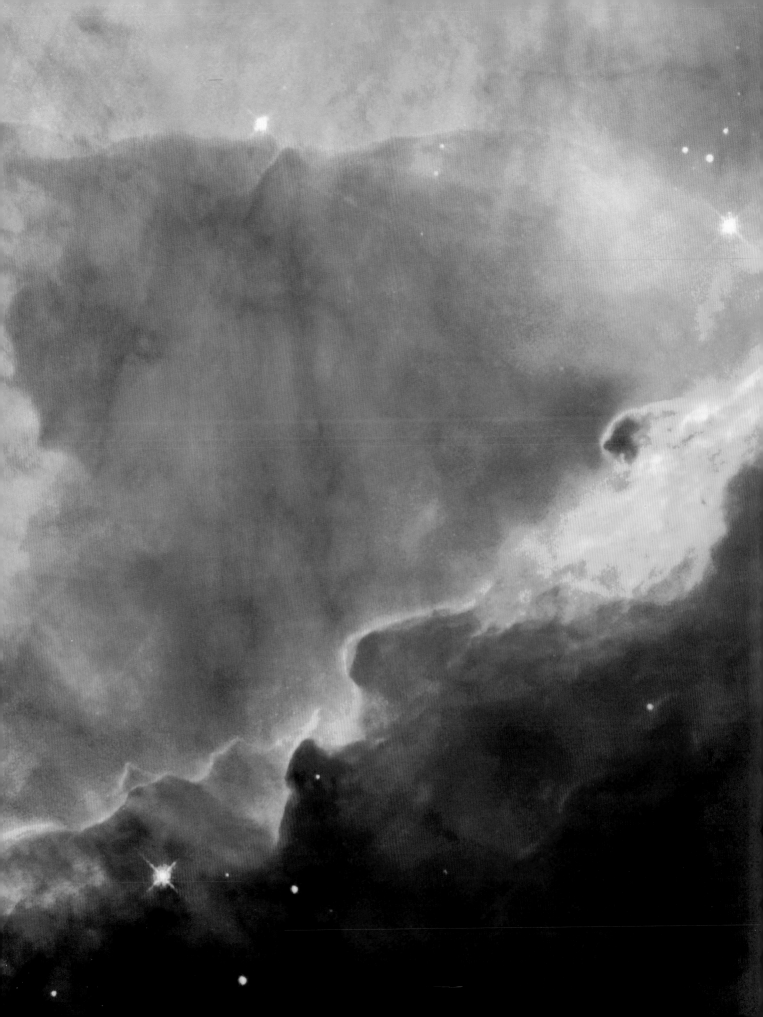

THE KABBALAH
A JEWISH MYSTICAL PATH

FRANJO TERHART

PaRragon

Bath · New York · Singapore · Hong Kong · Cologne · Delhi · Melbourne

This is a Parragon Publishing Book

Copyright © Parragon Books Ltd
Queen Street House
4 Queen Street
Bath BA1 1 HE, UK

Original edition: ditter.projektagentur Gmbh
Project coordinator: Irina Ditter-Hilkens
Copy editor: Kirsten E. Lehmann
Picture acquisition: Barbara Linz
Design and layout: Claudio Martinez

US edition produced by: APE Int'l.
Translation: Mary Dobrian

ISBN: 978-1-4054-8971-3

Printed in United Arab Emirates

CONTENTS

Theoretical Kabbalah 32

Practical Kabbalah 52

THE KABBALAH

Modern Kabbalists claim that reading Kabbalistic texts will energize practitioners—they will require less sleep, and feel happier and more well-balanced. Is this simply another new esoteric trend that began in the United States and has become increasingly popular in Europe in recent years? Far from it! The Kabbalah is anything but new—and was certainly not invented by preachers of esoteric healing. Rather, it is a millennia-old form of Jewish mysticism that has been known by this name for more than 800 years; a form of religious practice (also familiar to other belief systems) in which, through devotion and immersion, the faithful seek to personally experience a connection to God. The Kabbalah as it is handed down to us in the present day was given significant momentum by Spanish Jews of the thirteenth century, and Jewish mysticism has influenced the development of Judaism ever since that time. And once the ideas and beliefs of Jewish mysticism took hold in non-Jewish intellectual circles as well, particularly in Germany and Italy, a Christian form of Kabbalah even evolved.

Still today, there is an aura of mystery inherent in the Kabbalah. It encompasses not only a theoretical, mystical aspect, but a concrete, practical one as well. In practice, Kabbalists alternate between cosmological thought constructs and invocation of angels in direct requests for help. For this reason, Kabbalah is sometimes regarded as magic and at other times as philosophy. This quality of combining wise, timeless ideas with contemporary practice and meditative exercises has contributed to the fact that the Kabbalah is an absolute trendy in a great number of countries today.

The current Kabbalah boom

Not only pop icon Madonna, rock star Mick Jagger, and flashy pop siren Christina Aguilera, but also actress Elizabeth Taylor and soccer star David Beckham are adherents of the new Kabbalah movement. Following a riding accident, Madonna was sighted up to three times a day visiting the Kabbalah Center run by her

The Kabbalah leads the practitioner step by step toward understanding of God's creation. Anyone who wishes to embark upon this mystical path of Judaism should be aware that the Kabbalah contains a confusing multitude of theoretical and practical teachings.

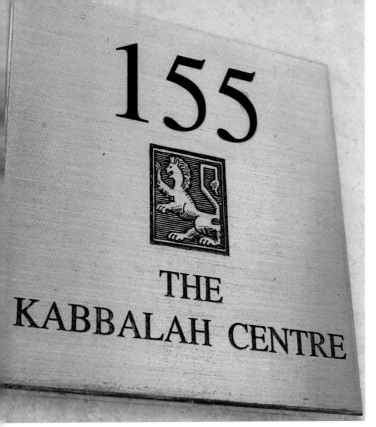

In recent years, numerous Kabbalah centers have been founded all over the world. Pictured here is the sign outside the Kabbalah Centre in New York City.

master, Yehuda Berg, to pray and meditate. With his bestselling book *The Power of Kabbalah*, Yehuda Berg revived public interest in this centuries-old mysticism—with the goal of making the Kabbalah accessible to everyone. According to a report in the Israeli newspaper *Maariv*, Berg has already founded over 40 Kabbalah Centers all over the world (for example, in Los Angeles, New York, Tel Aviv, Warsaw, and Pakistan).

Forgotten spiritual knowledge

Kabbalah (Hebrew: "receiving" or "received tradition") refers first of all to a body of texts that originated primarily in the Middle Ages, as well as in the early period of religious Judaism. The main text of the Kabbalah is the Zohar. This book is thought to have originated in Castile, Spain between 1275 and 1293; however, some Kabbalists believe the Zohar is considerably older. This rich source of spiritual knowledge had sunk increasingly into oblivion in the nineteenth century. In the age of the rising middle class and of Jewish emancipation, most of Europe's Jewish intellectuals frowned upon such practices as mysticism, meditation, and theosophical speculation. This attitude

changed in the twentieth century thanks to scholars such as Gershom Scholem and his pupil Moshe Idel. They rediscovered the Kabbalah as a significant religious-historical, epistemological, and scientific phenomenon.

The Kabbalah and the secrets of life

Since the second half of the twentieth century, there has also been renewed interest in the esoteric side of mystical Judaism. Today, many people feel drawn to the Kabbalah because it promises to reveal the great secrets of life: Why did the world come into being? What is the nature of the relationship between God and humans? Are there techniques through which it is possible to re-order life and make people happy?

The ancient, spiritual teachings of the Kabbalah are the subject of this book, which will trace its path from the beginnings of Jewish mysticism in the age of the patriarch Abraham up until the present day in a way that can be understood by everyone. The most important aspects of the theoretical, practical, and Christian Kabbalah will be introduced. These include the teachings of the great Kabbalistic sages as well as numerous examples from Kabbalistic practice.

English soccer player David Beckham is one of the many prominent devotees of the Kabbalah.

THE ORIGINS AND HISTORY OF
THE KABBALAH

The interior of the Dome of the Rock in Jerusalem, where, according to legend, Abraham prepared to sacrifice his son Isaac, and where the prophet Mohammed ascended into heaven on a horse-like creature. This site is also sacred to Kabbalists.

THE JEWISH FAITH

Judaism originated more than 3000 years ago; it is the oldest monotheistic religion in the world. According to its teachings, the God of the Hebrew scriptures (which corresponds to the Christian Old Testament) made an eternal covenant with his people, the Israelites. On Mount Sinai he gave them two tablets bearing the Ten Commandments, which became mandatory for the religion. All additional Jewish commandments, rituals, and duties—along with the history of the ancient Israelites—were recorded primarily in the Torah (see p. 15). Judaism does not include any belief in an afterlife; rather, there is the deep-seated hope that one day, the Messiah will appear who will transform all the people of the world into God's holy people. At the same time, the

evil people will be eradicated. The Israelites see themselves as the group chosen by God to set an example for all other peoples; all the rest will join them in the end.

The patriarch

The faithful consider Abraham (approx. 1900 BC) to be the progenitor of the Israelite nation and the ancestor of the tribe of Israel; at he same time, he is the first patriarch of his religion. Abraham left Mesopotamia, the land between the Euphrates and Tigris Rivers, and at God's behest, traveled with his clan and his herds as nomads until they reached the land of Canaan. God had promised to make Abraham the father of many offspring and of a great nation. Yet only in old age did Abraham's wife Sarah give birth to their son Isaac who, along with Jacob, Isaac's second son, plays an important role in Judaism. When God demanded that Abraham offer Isaac to him as a sacrifice, Abraham did not hesitate; in the end, however, the bloody deed was not carried out. According to Genesis 22, God had only wanted proof of Abraham's obedience.

Abraham, the first Kabbalist

As founder of the Jewish religion, Abraham is also considered the first Kabbalist, and his relationship to the Creator raises fundamental questions for followers of the Kabbalah. According to the Kabbalah, Abraham handed down the knowledge he acquired to succeeding generations. In the centuries that followed, the Kabbalah was passed on orally, and the successive great Kabbalists added their own personal experiences to the treasure trove of knowledge which they bequeathed and internalized. In later centuries, however, some Kabbalists also wondered how Abraham had communicated with God. What, exactly, were his methods and techniques? On this point, the patriarch was silent.

Kabbalists consider Abraham to have been the first of their number, since he had a direct relationship to God. However, he did not pass on the knowledge of how he communicated with God to succeeding generations of Kabbalists.

Jacob's dream of a ladder between heaven and earth became a symbol of the human quest for a way to leave the earthly sphere and ascend to God.

Jacob's ladder
Along with Abraham, Jacob—the son of Isaac—is another important figure in the early history of the Kabbalah. Following a disagreement with his brother Esau, Jacob was forced to flee. The Bible says that one night, a vision of angels on a ladder appeared to him in a dream. The ladder reached from the earth to heaven and God (Genesis 28).

For some Kabbalists and for secret societies—for example, the mystical Order of the Golden Dawn (see p. 77)—this ladder became a symbol of ascension into supernatural worlds. In his mind, Jacob created a connection between the world above and the one below, in the form of a ladder. The Kabbalists who followed and emulated him sought to use this ladder as an aid to meditation as well as a magical tool. After all, mystical Kabbalah is concerned with exactly this: the ascension of the soul to God. According to Kabbalists, Jacob was thus the first person to practice this act in his mind.

MOSES AND ELIJAH

Moses led the Israelites out of bondage in Egypt and made a covenant with God. Through Moses, the Israelites received the Ten Commandments. He is an agent between human beings and God, and the first five books of scripture are named after him: the Books of Moses. Moses is the only person who spoke with God "face to face"—even though God's face was hidden in a fire (Exodus 3). God also told Moses his real name: "I AM THAT I AM." Kabbalists have pondered this enigmatic sentence—which Moses apparently understood—for thousands of years: What statement did God want to make about himself? Others wonder who the founder of the Jewish religion really was. Was the historical Moses an Egyptian? To this day, archeologists and Biblical scholars continue to search for clues about his life.

A freedom fighter, circa 1300 BC?

Some Egyptologists speculate that Moses could have been Amunmasesa, an Egyptian deputy ruler from the thirteenth century BC, who led an uprising against the Pharaoh. The Bible, the Egyptologists hypothesize, recorded memories of the rebellion and retold the story. Thus, the Egyptian became an Israelite, and the leader of the rebellion against the pharaoh became a freedom fighter. Today, scholars widely assume that Egyptian ideas also contributed to the Biblical belief in a single God. Even before Moses' time, Pharaoh Akhenaten (ca. 1360 BC) had abolished all the deities with the exception of one—the sun god Aten—in a religious revolution. Akhenaten's teachings stated that that God reached out to humankind through love.

The prophet Elijah demonstrates the power of the God of Israel to an assembled crowd. Kabbalists and religious Jews honor Elijah as an opponent of the cult of Baal and an ardent champion of monotheistic belief in Yahweh.

Moses, too, was constantly forced to combat the Israelites' lack of faith. Thus, according to legend, in his rage over the people's unbridled dancing and revelry around the golden calf—a graven idol—he smashed the tablets containing the Ten Commandments on the ground.

Elijah's mysterious powers

The prophet Elijah lived in the first half of the ninth century BC, and is also counted among the founding fathers of the Kabbalah. He possessed extraordinary powers and abilities. Among other things, he is said to have ridden up to heaven in a "chariot of fire" (2 Kings 2). His contacts with God were quite unusual: in a contest with other prophets to determine the identity of the one true God, he prayed together with the others on Mount Carmel. Each of the prophets had prepared a sacrificial altar in the hope that God would accept it by setting it on fire. This did indeed occur— but only on Elijah's altar (1 Kings 18).

Following the death of this revered prophet, he was carried up to heaven in a fiery chariot. This image is still used today to symbolize a great prophet or a God-fearing person. The Talmud calls Elijah "God's representative." Among Kabbalists, he is considered to be one of the great sages whom God favored with especially close contact.

The Torah and the revival of the Kabbalah

The compilation of the Torah (another name for the Five Books of Moses)—whose text, the faithful believe, was dictated by God himself—brought with it a new movement in the evolution of the Kabbalah. As early as 586–515 BC, groups of people studied the Kabbalah; and following the destruction of the Temple of Jerusalem in the year 70 AD by the Romans, the development of the Kabbalah continued. At the same time, the first important texts concerned with methods of instruction in the Kabbalah were composed. In the second century AD, Rabbi Simeon bar Yohai became a major figure in the renewal of the Kabbalah. Rabbi Simeon bar Yohai, in turn, was a pupil of Rabbi Akiva (40–132 AD). Akiva and many of his followers were tortured and killed by the Romans, who felt threatened by the teachings of the Kabbalah.

The Torah rolls are sacred to Jews, an attitude that stems from their belief that the words on the srolls are God's own words. When they become old and worn out, they are not thrown away, but buried.

SIMEON BAR YOHAI

During the suppression of the Jewish "Bar Kokhba" revolt against the Roman authority in Palestine (132–135 AD), only Rabbi Simeon bar Yohai and four other rabbis were able to escape the Roman massacre. They sought refuge in a cave and remained hidden there for 13 years. According to a legend that endures to this day, the Zohar—the most important book of the Kabbalah—was written here. The legend tells us that Rabbi Simeon bar Yohai lived through and mastered all of the mystical 125 steps that a person can attain during his or her lifetime on this earth. In addition, two predictions attributed to bar Yohai have been passed down to us. The first of these states that one day, even a six-year-old child could have access to the spiritual knowledge of the Kabbalah. The second says that the text bar Yohai composed would remain secret for a period of exactly 1200 years. It was Moses de León in Spain who made a significant contribution to the compilation of the main text of the Kabbalah, the *Zohar* (Hebrew: "splendor," "radiance") beginning in 1270 and up until its publication in 1290—more than 1200 years after the destruction of the Temple of Jerusalem in the year 70 AD. One could, if one wished, interpret this time period as the fulfillment of Simeon bar Yohai's prophecy.

After the destruction of the Temple in the year 70 AD, Beth She'arim became a refuge for the Jewish community from Roman oppression. The grave of Rabbi Judah—who, around 200 AD, was the first person to record sections of the Talmud in writing—is also located here.

The purpose of the theoretical Kabbalah since Rabbi Simeon's time

The purpose of the Kabbalah since Simeon bar Yohai's time has been to uncover God's inner being, from which everything else originates. The Kabbalah can be understood as a source of concealed wisdom—a store of all spiritual knowledge and teachings—through which all the secrets of the universe can be deciphered. It claims to contain the answers to all the questions that plague humankind. Only the secret name of the Creator, the Kabbalah says, may never be revealed.

THE MAJOR SOURCES OF THE KABBALAH

The body of knowledge we identify as the Kabbalah includes a great many texts that record theoretical ideas about the nature of God, heaven and earth, the nature of human beings, and our potential to recognize the truth. The first systematic compilation of Kabbalistic thought took place over 1000 years ago in Catalonia, Spain and Provence, France. Its precursors were ancient mystical sources that had been in circulation for centuries, pondered by countless Jewish scholars and philosophers, and passed on from generation to generation.

Throughout the centuries, Kabbalists have continually discovered messages in the Torah which remain concealed from uninformed readers of the sacred texts.

The Torah and the Talmud

The two main writings of the Jewish religion are the Torah (the Five Books of Moses, also called the Pentateuch, from the Greek *penta* = "five") and the Talmud. The Torah is considered to be a divine revelation that Moses received on Mount Sinai; it is the basis of the ethical and ritual commandments of Judaism. The Torah contains 613 separate commandments (mitzvoth), which are subdivided into 248 "positive commandments" and 365 "negative commandments," or commands to abstain. By observing these commandments, faithful Jews can direct their lives toward God.

The Talmud is the second major work. It contains Jewish religious law. The Talmud is divided into two parts: the Mishnah, which was set down in writing by Rabbi Judah in Israel around 200 AD, and the Gemara, which was completed around the year 500 and consists of commentary on the Mishnah. There are a Jerusalem Talmud and a Babylonian Talmud, each of which is named after the place where it was drafted. The Babylonian Talmud is generally considered the more significant of the two.

THE HEBREW ALPHABET

Name	Hebrew symbol	Transcription (English)	Numerical value
Alef	א	a	(1)
Bet	ב	b	(2)
Gimel	ג	g	(3)
Dalet	ד	d	(4)
He	ה	h	(5)
Vav	ו	v, w	(6)
Zajin	ז	z	(7)
Khet	ח	kh	(8)
Tet	ט	t	(9)
Yod	י	y	(10)
Kaf/Khaf	כ	k, kh	(20)
Lamed	ל	l	(30)
Mem	מ	m	(40)
Nun	נ	n	(50)
Samekh	ס	s	(60)
Ayin	ע	' (*)	(70)
Pe, Fe	פ	p, f	(80)
Tsadi	צ	ts	(90)
Kuf	ק	k (q)	(100)
Resh	ר	r	(200)
Shin, Sin	ש	sh, s	(300)
Tav	ת	t	(400)

(*) a guttural sound with no equivalent in the Roman alphabet

The Hebrew alphabet is the starting point for the theoretical study of the Kabbalah. Without this alphabet—which consists of 22 symbols—there would be no Kabbalah. For Kabbalists, the 22 letters, each of which is assigned a numerical value, are instruments of creation in the sense in which they are put into effect in the Book of Genesis (the book of Creation in the Bible). Here, when God says "Let there be light!," it is said in Hebrew.

Thus, a person who meditates on the Hebrew letters is speaking with God. If that person combines the letters with one another, then he or she is combining numbers and letters at the same time. Each individual letter is connected to the creative forces of the universe. Therefore, they can be employed as magical formulas—and this is why the first words of the Hebrew Bible are so significant: *Bereshit bara Elohim* … ("In the beginning God created …"). God, however, is not called by his true name, since this name should not be dishonored by human beings; rather, the word "Elohim" expresses a plural concept.

The Hebrew language

The importance accorded to language in the scriptures can be more clearly illustrated with the following example. In (ancient) Hebrew the word *behemah*—"cattle"—has the same root as the word that means "to be poor in speech/devoid of speech." Thus, it also expresses a significant difference between humans and animals: animals are capable of making sounds and can communicate to a certain degree, but compared to human beings, they are dumb. In Judaism, human beings are the only creatures acknowledged to have the power of speech.

In order to further understand the Hebrew language and its peculiarities, one must keep in mind that it belongs to the family of Semitic languages, which includes Syriac, Aramaic, and various others, along with numerous Arabic dialects. In these languages, three consonants frequently form the basis of a word. These consonants remain recognizable as the root of all of that word's linguistic variations and grammatical forms. Here are two examples, each containing three basic consonants—in Romanized transcriptions of the Hebrew letters—which take on new meanings through modifications of the words:

1) m-l-kh: melekh—king; malkha—queen; malakh—[he] ruled, but also: [he] consulted, etc.
2) s-f-r: sefer—book; sifrut—literature; sefora—numeral/number; mispar—calculation of time; sfira—sphere (in the Kabbalah); [hu] sofer—[he is] a writer, but also: [he] counts, etc.

The classification of the alphabet by numbers

Kabbalists explain that the letters Alef through Yod denote the invisible world—the world of angels. The letter Kaf through the letter Ayin signify various groups of angelic beings that inhabit the visible world. The letters Pe through Tav indicate the world that is assigned to the spirit. This is the inner being that gives a life and soul to all creatures. The numerical values of the letters are as follows:

1. Alef (1), Bet (2), Gimel (3), Dalet (4), He (5), Vav (6), Zayin (7), Khet (8), Tet (9), Yod (10)
2. Kaf (20), Lamed (30), Mem (40), Nun (50), Samekh (60), Ayin (70)
3. Pe/Fe (80), Tsadi (90), Kuf (100), Resh (200), Shin (300), Tav (400)

The special meanings of certain letters
Alef represents the first name of God. Kabbalists call God "the one whom the eye has never seen." His attribute is the crown or the diadem. Bet is the second name of God. It denotes the angels of the second order, the Cherubim. The hierarchy of angels ends with Yod, in the invisible world; Ayin completes the world of the Archangels (e.g. Michael). Kof signifies the earth; Tav corresponds to the microcosmos, the third divine principle. It symbolizes human beings, because it signifies the purpose of everything that exists: humans are considered the highest achievement in all creation.

The unspeakable name of God
YHWH is the Latin transcription of the Hebrew word which means God; it is also called the Tetragrammaton, in reference to its four letters. For faithful Jews, there is a taboo against ever speaking the word "Yahweh" out loud. Thus in prayer, rabbis speak of God as "The holy One, blessed is He." In this way, God's holy status is preserved and his name is not reduced to the mundane level of earthly things. Adonai (my Lord) and Elohim Zebaoth (Lord of Hosts) are some of the other transcriptions used for God. According to Jewish belief, the Hebrew name of God attests to the fact that the Creation is an all-encompassing event of names and language. A person who knows the true names and their numerical values is a Kabbalist.

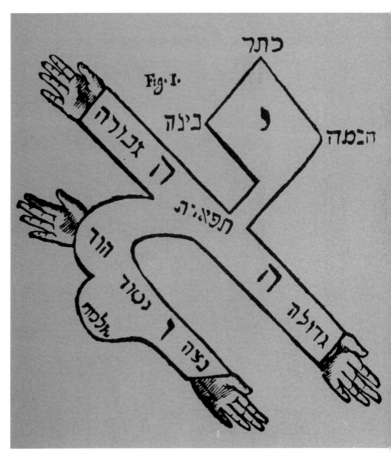

The letter Alef is the beginning of all existence. According to the Kabbalah, it was the first letter that appeared before God, in order that the world might be created.

THE BOOK ZOHAR

The primary text of the Kabbalah is the Zohar, a book of mystical teachings that originated in Spain in the thirteenth century. It is written in the form of parables in Aramaic, which is the language spoken by Jesus of Nazareth. The Zohar regards Aramaic as the reverse side of Hebrew—by this, it means its hidden side. The very fact that the Zohar was not written in Hebrew demonstrates to religious Jews that it is the work of human beings, in contrast to the Torah.

According to one legend, Simeon bar Yohai supposedly hid the texts of the Zohar in a cave near Safed on Lake Genesareth (also called the Sea of Galilee), where they were only discovered centuries later by Arabs who had settled in the area. A further anecdote describes how the Zohar was recognized by skillful eyes: One day, a Kabbalist from Safed bought some fish from an Arab fishmonger at the marketplace and to his tremendous astonishment recognized the true value of the paper in which the fish were wrapped. He subsequently purchased all the Arab vendor's remaining pieces of paper and compiled them together into a book: the Zohar.

The town of Safed is located to the north of Lake Genesareth in Israel. For many generations of Kabbalists, Safed was their most important religious center.

The mystical textbook of the Kabbalah is the Zohar. It attempts to comprehend the nature of God and to make it accessible to human beings.

Moses de León

Historians of the Kabbalah assume that Rabbi Moses de León (1250–1305) was the first person to compile the ideas and beliefs of the Kabbalah—some of which may well have been available to him in writing—and in the thirteenth century, in Spain, was the first to publish them. The Zohar is considered to be a collection of all Kabbalistic teachings from the first century to the present; it consists of 2400 densely written pages in the Aramaic language. Moses de León denied that he was the original author of the Zohar; however, no one has ever seen the original text, reputedly written by Simeon bar Yohai.

Simeon bar Yohai is said to have hidden the original version of the Zohar in a cave near the city of Safed.

The interplay of light and shadow can be seen as a modern, symbolic depiction of the Sefirot, since it expresses the interconnection between the (positive) Sefirot and the (negative) Klifah.

The essence of the Zohar

The Zohar works from the assumption of a period of human development covering 6000 years, beginning with the Creation. During this period, souls pass through a dynamic process, from generation to generation. At the end of the process the souls reach the "End of Correction"—the highest state of spirituality and perfection. Of paramount importance to the Kabbalah are the ten divine Sefirot—emanations or channels of the one indivisible God, which bring happiness and blessings to people and their lives. However, the Zohar is also concerned with the hierarchy of evil—the so-called unholy Sefirot; they stand in sharp contrast to the divine world of light.

God's ten "steps"
"Sefirot" is one of the most important basic terms in the Kabbalah. It refers to the ten qualities of the Absolute, the Most High—Ein Sof, equivalent to the unknown, mysterious God. The ten Sefirot can best be imagined as ten branches of a large tree; they bear the radiance or emanations of God. These branches form the various steps of divine existence, through which the hidden world of the Absolute—that is, God—becomes visible. The individual steps (Sefira) are, from top to bottom:

1. Kether = Crown of the deity 2. Chokhmah = Wisdom, or the original idea of God 3. Binah = God's intelligence 4. Chesed = God's love or mercy 5. Gevurah = Power or judgment 6. Tifereth = Compassion or beauty 7. Netzach = Endurance or eternity 8. Hod = God's majesty 9. Yesod = Basis or foundation of all of God's active and creative powers 10. Malkuth = God's kingdom.
These ten Sefirot are interconnected by 22 paths or channels of energy (see p. 40), corresponding to the number of letters in the Hebrew alphabet.

God and the world

Kabbalists use the ten Sefirot to illustrate for themselves the ways in which God, as an eternal and incorporeal being—who is also infinite and utterly unfathomable to the human mind—is able to interact with human beings, whose abilities are so minimal in comparison. God radiates into the world through the Sefirot and thus imparts some concept of his own being to the people. The human being stands at the bottom, at the roots of the tree; Malkuth means God's kingdom as seen from a human perspective, as well as the present and the foundation or beginning of everything. From here, a person can embark on a journey to grasp the nature of God. The ten Sefirot are divided into equal numbers of male and female aspects of God (see p. 41), called *Partzufim* (faces): God's ten different aspects or emanations simultaneously reflect aspects of human beings because the latter were created by God in God's own image. Kabbalists are concerned with intellectual as well as emotional interactions with God; both of these spheres comprise characteristics of the Creator, and are reflected as such in human beings.

The energy channels

Twenty-two energy channels connect the Sefirot to one another. Each of these energy channels corresponds to a particular Hebrew letter (see p. 40). Meditations on individual letters of these connecting paths between the Sefirot can help people regain their lost equilibrium; the Sefirot, in turn, help them to better understand themselves and God. Everything in the universe is connected with everything else—and human beings are a part of it. Thus, for example, in the Zohar, human anger and aggression are attributed to Gevurah, or power. The energy channel that connects power to love (Chesed) bears the letter Alef. Therefore, the Kabbalah advises followers to meditate on the letter Alef in order to overcome aggression.

How can a person find a path to God? This is a fundamental question of the Kabbalah. We must think of Jewish mysticism as a centuries-old field of experience in which generations of Kabbalists have learned and applied knowledge that has been passed down.

The Cathedral of León still dominates the city today. Here, in all probability, Moses de León wrote the Zohar, thus making the Kabbalah known beyond the narrowest circles of the initiated.

The Zohar—a perennial source of controversy among Kabbalists

The Zohar is an extraordinary collection of texts, and the most complete and important book of teachings in the Kabbalah. Jewish mysticism achieves its apex in the Zohar, since nothing which has been written since—all the way up to the present day—has been able to approach the genius of its ideas. From time immemorial Kabbalists have attempted to determine who the true author of the Zohar was, and for centuries speculation has arisen from the fact that the mystery of its origin has never been unequivocally solved. One group of Kabbalists continues to assume that the Zohar can be traced back to Simeon bar Yohai in the second century. The other, larger faction of Kabbalistic scholars, however, believes that Moses de León was the author of the Zohar, and the evidence that they present for this case

is indisputably significant. One of the first scholars who attempted to determine the work's authorship was Isaac ben Samuel of Acre (around 1305). He questioned Moses de León directly about the Zohar.

The widow of Moses de León

Moses de León promised to show the original hand-written texts of the Zohar to his colleague from Acre; however, he died unexpectedly soon afterwards. Isaac ben Samuel subsequently visited the widow of the deceased rabbi, who told him that no such book written by Simeon bar Yohai existed. Her husband, she said, was the actual author, inspired by God. According to her, Moses de León had already discovered the magical word for God and—upon hearing his name—the Most High had presented him with the text of the Zohar. Why had her husband not confessed to being the author? Because everyone would have thought he was a fantasist, but if the text were attributed to the wise Kabbalist Simeon bar Yohai, people would certainly place their faith in all of the wisdom that the book contained.

Revival of the Kabbalah through the Zohar

The first writer to refer to the Zohar was the Italian Kabbalist Menahem Recanati (around 1320). In his "Sefer Taamei Hamitzvot," an interpretation of religious law, he quotes the Zohar numerous times. The Zohar itself was first printed in 1588 in the Italian city of Cremona. With its publication, the productive energy of Kabbalistic ideas appeared to have been exhausted. All Kabbalists after Moses de León studied the Zohar, wrote treatises on individual subjects, and attempted to apply them. Initially, the Zohar was met with resistance, particularly on the part of Talmudists, since the Zohar itself appears to be a Bible of the Kabbalah; they thus saw it as a rival to the Talmud. The Kabbalists asserted that they possessed the key to the secrets of the universe, and even more: using the Zohar, they could now unambiguously interpret all of the previously impenetrable passages of the holy Torah. Statements such as this provoked strong resistance among devout Talmudists. Nevertheless, the Zohar's growing influence on Judaism could not be stopped.

Acre (Akko) was once a Crusader city in the Holy Land. It was the home of Isaac ben Samuel, who attempted to determine the origins of the Zohar. Upon speaking with the widow of Moses de León, he learned that the Zohar was most likely not written in the Holy Land, but rather in Spain.

The beginning of the Zohar
In its opening passages, the book appears dark and mysterious, yet reveals the great fascination of this work: "With the beginning of the manifestation of the King's will, THAT IS, WHEN THE KING DESIRED TO CREATE THE WORLD, a hard spark made an engraving upon the supernal light..." It goes on to describe how colors developed from nothingness, breaking free from a certain point and emanating out into the universe. These sparks or rays evolved into the ten Sefirot. Behind this point, however, lies the most hidden of all hidden things, which is sealed off from human perception.

The Zohar is written in a mysterious style and is full of mystical images. A human stands at the foot of the Sefirot tree, while the crown—Kether— flows from the unfathomable Ein Sof, the unknowable circle of God's light.

CREATION MYTHS

Like all people who believe in a creator God, Kabbalists assume the preexistence of God, who set the process of Creation in motion. God created the universe out of a void (compare the Latin phrase *creatio ex nihilo*—creation out of nothingness). But what exactly did God do after the Creation? After creating the world, did he then withdraw from it, and through his absence, make it possible for evil to enter? Jewish mystics and Kabbalists vehemently reject this idea. For them, God and the universe are one and the same thing. However, some Kabbalists believe that God preserves the universe, but that he himself is nevertheless removed from it in a certain way. According to the Bahir—which, next to the Zohar, is the second most important book in the Kabbalah—God layered matter onto himself. Thus, the entire world is made up of God, even though we human beings only ever see a single surface.

"The beginning created God," writes the author of the Zohar mysteriously. This statement makes God Himself the creation of a powerful principle which is inconceivable to human understanding.

The ideas of the Zohar
Genesis relates, "In the beginning God created …"; the Zohar says, "The beginning created God …". In the Zohar, God is Ein Sof, the fundamental principle, which remains eternally immaterial and unrecognizable to humans. By means of channeled energy, Ein Sof created Elohim, the God within our universe. This type of subordinate deity is called a demiurge. Elohim, in turn, created heaven and earth, as told in the Bible. According to the Zohar, Creation was initiated through sacred words: ten times God said: "Let there be …" In this process, the ten Sefirot came into being, as radiations or emanations of God. Thus, the Kabbalah interprets the God of the Bible as a subordinate God—and mystical stories have been passed down in which God does not know this …

SEFER YETZIRAH, THE BOOK OF CREATION

The *Sefer Yetzirah* (Hebrew: "Book of Creation") is the oldest book of the early Kabbalah that was written in Hebrew. Its authorship is unknown. It originated around the middle of the first millennium in Palestine and exists in two different versions, one longer and one shorter. It contains fundamental mystical ideas, including the concept of the ten Sefirot. During the period around 1000 AD, the Sefer Yetzirah was commented on more frequently than any other mystical text—in part because it claims to date back to Abraham. It is primarily concerned with the Hebrew alphabet and the ten Sefirot; together, these two groups of symbols make up the "32 secret paths" of which the Sefer tells: it is the task of the human being to discover them.

Three levels of existence

The book specifies the three levels upon which the world exists: the levels of writing, of speech, and of numbers. The three levels allow people to follow different, interlacing paths in order to experience the spiritual and material worlds. As previously explained here (see p. 17), each letter in the Hebrew alphabet is assigned a numerical value, so that the world and all objects and events are registered by their numerals as well as by their names. In this system, the three so-called "mother letters"—Alef (1), Mem (40), and Shin (300)—play a special role, since in their respective symbolic meanings—namely air, water, and fire—they are the fundamental elements that stabilize the universe. Consequently, a person who meditates on these letters can experience inner stability and equilibrium. Nevertheless, even skilled Kabbalists acknowledge that the book Sefer Yetzirah is extremely difficult to interpret. The most important commentaries on the Sefer Yetzirah were written by the Hebrew poet Yehuda Halevi (1075–1141).

According to the Kabbalah, the universe originated through the power of the ten Sefirot, which in turn sprung from the fundamental principle—Ein Sof. This process of creation out of nothingness corresponds with modern perceptions about the universe.

THE BAHIR

Some time between the appearance of the Sefer Yetzirah and publication of the Zohar in the late thirteenth century, the *Bahir*—the "Book of Brightness"—was written. According to legend, it is much older: it is said to have been written by Rabbi Nehunya Ben Ha-Kanah in the first century AD, but was only discovered in the twelfth century. The Bahir mainly addresses the creation of the world and humans, as well as good and evil (here we see the influence of Gnostic teachings). Two powers rule the universe: a benevolent God and an evil, arrogant power that opposes God. However, since Judaism teaches that God cannot be overpowered by anything in the universe, this evil power is perceived as one that constantly challenges him, albeit not as an enemy. Rather, the Bahir explains that there is a positive as well as a negative quality attributable to each of the ten Sefirot. In order to reach the truth—that is, God's light—one must attempt to free oneself from the world.

The Bahir prescribes fasting, prayer, and meditation as the best methods for doing so. In addition, the book speaks of the transmigration of souls in the sense of "reused" souls: things a person experiences in life have their roots in a previous life. In this way, the Bahir also provides an explanation for human suffering. The text was initially read and studied in southern France, but quickly moved into wider circulation.

A story from the Bahir

Rabbi Rachumai explained to his pupils that the light—the human soul (which recognizes God's truth)—existed even before the creation of the universe. His pupils did not understand. The rabbi continued, "Imagine that a king wishes for a son with all his heart. One day he discovers a beautiful crown. 'This crown will be for my son,' he thinks, and he keeps it. Other people ask him, 'But King, how do you know that your son will be worthy of this crown?' The king then responds: 'Shush! I specifically created my universe this way ...'"

This old Jewish archive in Seville, Spain contains important hand-written texts concerning the Kabbalah. Researchers from all over the world visit this archive to examine valuable writings on a wide range of subjects in Jewish history.

In Provence, Rabbi Isaac the Blind set down the first practical instructions in the history of the Kabbalah.

THE HEYDAY OF THE KABBALAH IN NORTHERN SPAIN AND PROVENCE

The presence of Judaism in Spain contributed significantly to the development of both alchemy and the Kabbalah, particularly in northern Spain, and not least thanks to centuries of contact with Islam during the rule of the Moors from the eighth to the fifteenth centuries. Beginning in 1492, all Jews were driven out of Spain and Portugal; they settled mainly in North Africa, Italy, and the Middle East. In Provence, Rabbi Isaac the Blind (Rabbi Yitzhak Saggi Nehor, 1160–1236) became known as an important Kabbalist. He taught that people can experience God in meditation if the energy of the ten Sefirot "passes through" them. For the first time in the history of the Kabbalah, Isaac the Blind's writings contained many practical instructions. His teachings, however, were in blatant contrast to the dominant views of Judaism at that time, which held that "power" could be achieved only through the practice of rituals and the study of the Torah.

The Kabbalist Abraham Abulafia

The Kabbalist Abraham Abulafia (1240–1291)—a native of Zaragoza who worked and taught in Spain as well as Italy, Greece, and Israel—also developed physical exercises and meditation techniques. He was of the opinion that people must not only recognize God, but experience him as well.

For Abraham Abulafia, too, all meditation begins with the Sefirot. According to his theories, not only can individuals further their spiritual development, but in fact, a great number of people who are schooled in the Kabbalah can join together to keep evil at bay from the world. His practical instructions, which can still be read in the Sefer Yetzirah, are somewhat reminiscent of Yoga techniques: "Raise both your arms over your head; the fingertips should touch each other; lower your arms as if you were chopping wood."

In 1270, Abulafia had a vision in which he received an order to meet with Pope Nicholas III (1210–1280). Ten years later, he attempted to meet with the pope, but was turned away under the threat of being burned at the stake. Abulafia disregarded the threat and journeyed to the Pope's country estate in Soriano, Italy. Just as he arrived, the Pope died unexpectedly—an event that saved Abulafia's life. He subsequently traveled to Sicily and taught there until his death.

The Kabbalah's Second Period of Development

In the centuries that followed, understanding of the Kabbalah was influenced most strongly by the theories of the most important Kabbalist of all: Rabbi Isaac Luria (1534–1572), also called the Ari, or the lion. Isaac Luria was originally raised in Jerusalem, but after his father died his mother brought him to his uncle's house in Egypt, where he developed an interest in the Kabbalah. Legend has it that he spent seven years alone on the island of Roda on the Nile, studying the Zohar. In 1569, Ari traveled to Safed—the center of Kabbalistic study at that time—where he lived with Moses Cordovero (1522–1570), a famous rabbi of the period, and read his book, the Ramak. After his master's death, Luria took over his position, and soon earned great acclaim as a mystic and a modernizer of the Kabbalah. Singing and joyousness, meditation and lively

Prayer and ecstasy

Rabbi Isaac Luria introduced an ecstatic form of worship that included singing and laughter. To him, dance and heartfelt prayer were not contradictory. In addition, he encouraged his followers to dedicate each action of their everyday lives—be it religious or profane—to God. He believed that everything human beings do is reflected on a spiritual level.

The grave of Rabbi Ari in Safed, Israel, is sought out and honored by both Orthodox Jews (as shown here) and modern Kabbalists alike. Safed is also believed to be the place where Rabbi Simeon bar Yohai primarily lived and worked in the second century.

The grave of the most important Kabbalist, Rabbi Isaac Luria, is located in the north of Safed. Many Kabbalists regularly make pilgrimages to the site and light candles there in his honor.

conversation were the means he used to disseminate knowledge about the Kabbalah; thanks to Luria, the Kabbalah became accessible to wider sections of the population for the first time. The Ari's gravesite in Safed, Israel continues to be a popular place of pilgrimage to this day.

The writings of Isaac Luria

Chaim Vital (1542–1620) was a pupil and close confidant of Luria's. He was the first to record Luria's ideas in writing (Luria himself died young and had written very little) and saw himself as the guardian of the Ari's spiritual legacy. At the same time, however, Chaim Vital was a respected Kabbalistic scholar in his own right, as well as a rabbi in Jerusalem and Damascus. He preserved Isaac Luria's theories in two books, which became known as *Etz HaChaim* ("The Tree of Life") and *Etz HaDaat* ("The Tree of Knowledge"). The fundamental idea of the Lurian Kabbalah is that through one's own actions, a person becomes the master of his or her own fate. Additional aspects of Isaac Luria's Kabbalah will be introduced in further chapters of this book (see p. 32ff.).

Sabbatai Zewi—a dubious messiah

More than a few Kabbalists believed themselves to be the promised Messiah who would bring salvation to the people of Israel. The most famous of these was Sabbatai Zewi (1626–1676), who declared himself the savior of his people. He, too, studied the Ari's writings; however, he also openly violated Jewish law. Nevertheless, he acquired a large following who believed that Sabbatai was the Messiah. The Messianic movement of "Sabbatianism" was widespread primarily in the Ottoman Empire and in Poland; elements of the movement were preserved in Chassidism. In 1666, Ottoman authorities presented Sabbatai Zewi with the choice of being executed or converting to Islam; Sabbatai chose to convert. From then on, he is said to have lived in the sultan's palace as a Muslim, but secretly he continued to practice Judaism. Due to the persistent activity of his followers, the false messiah was finally arrested and banished in 1672.

Kabbalah is philosophical and theological theory, but it is by no means limited to prayer and meditation. Dancing and singing, laughter and ecstatic demonstrations of friendship are also part of it.

A Hasidic rabbi enters an old synagogue in Safed. In 1530, the Jewish poet and Kabbalist Shlomo Alkabetz wrote the mystical prayer "Lekhah Dodi" (Come, My Beloved) here, which is still sung to this day.

HASIDISM AND THE HASIDIM

Hasidism (Hebrew: *hasid*—"the pious") developed in protest against the official rabbinism, as a reform movement among Eastern European Jews. In Hasidism, it was no longer the intellectually-minded rabbi—who emphasized terms like mercy, holiness, and love—who played a major role, but rather the tzaddik, an intermediary between the earthly and the divine spheres. The Hasidim wanted to bring new life to their religion, which they felt had become paralyzed by laws and commandments, above all through spirituality, mysticism, and magic. Precursors of the Hasidim had already existed in the Rhineland in the twelfth and thirteenth centuries (German Hasidism); however, their ideas and practices were more bound up with strict self-castigation. The founder of Eastern European Hasidism was Rabbi Israel ben Eliezer (1700–1760), better known by the title Ba'al Shem Tov. This extraordinary man was an itinerant preacher, Kabbalist, and miracle worker who perceived the divine in every aspect of the world.

The Ba'al Shem Tov and the mystical flight of the soul

The Ba'al Shem Tov believed that God exists within the world, which is simply his vestment. The Kabbalistic statement "there is no place without him" is the starting point for Hasidic teachings, in which God and people look one another in the eye. According to the Ba'al Shem Tov (who is said to have been able to heal deathly ill people) humans are intended to achieve a complete grasp of the essence of life. This is best accomplished through mystical flight of the soul, in order to reach the "higher" worlds, according to the Kabbalistic understanding of the hierarchical order of the cosmos. Through a state of ecstasy, he said, in which the soul rises above the body, we can penetrate all of creation, and the inner connection between all creatures and things becomes visible. Only when a person can see that death does not exist can he or she become free.

CHRISTIAN INTEREST IN THE KABBALAH IN THE MIDDLE AGES

In the Middle Ages, the Kabbalah was a means of religious cognition available only to educated Jews, especially since knowledge of Hebrew was required to read the texts. Europe's Christian intellectual circles only began to study Hebrew at the end of the fifteenth century, when Christian theologians wished to translate the Bible not only from Greek and Latin, but from Hebrew as well. Little by little, certain philosophers, theologians, and writers became interested in Jewish mystical traditions and thus encountered the Kabbalah. One such scholar was the German humanist Johann Reuchlin (1455–1522), who, along with Italian philosopher Pico della Mirandola (1463–1494), was introduced to the correlations contained in the Kabbalah during their meeting with Jewish scholars in Venice in 1490. Reuchlin not only published several books about Jewish mysticism— among them *De verbo mirifico* (On the Miraculous Word, 1494) and *De arte cabbalistica* (The Art of Kabbalism, 1517)—but a book of Hebrew grammar as well. Writing in the form of a learned discourse between four sages, Reuchlin combined a Platonic understanding of the world and Pythagorean philosophy with Christian beliefs and the Kabbalah.

Agrippa von Nettesheim

The natural philosopher Agrippa von Nettesheim (1486–1535), a native of Cologne, studied the Kabbalah and taught that God created the world out of nothingness as a reflection of his ideas. These ideas emanate from him like rays, and are reminiscent of the ten Sefirot. Here, human beings are at the center point between three worlds: the supernatural world of angels, the celestial world of the stars' movement, and the world of earthly elements. Thus, the human soul consists of three parts: reason, sensation, and vegetative existence. Kabbalists interpreted this the same way, as reflected in their significant terms, "neshamah, ruach, and nephesh" (see p. 36).

R. Cooper sculp.t

HENRICUS CORNELIUS AGRIPPA.

The teachings of Agrippa von Nettesheim, which were strongly influenced by the Kabbalah, can be summed up as follows: God rules the world, but his will is executed by his servants, which also include demons.

THEORETICAL
KABBALAH

THE DOCTRINE OF THE SUPREME BEING AND THE UNIVERSE

The theoretical Kabbalah focuses primarily on two thematic areas: the doctrine of the supreme being—that is, God or Ein Sof—and the universe or space, i.e. the macrocosmos. Both of these realms are particularly illuminating with regard to understanding the soul (the psychology of human beings) and behavior (questions of human ethics).

Over the centuries, the great Kabbalists have repeatedly examined these themes. Of these, Isaac Luria, with his ideas about the respective natures of God and of human beings, probably made the strongest and most lasting impact on the Kabbalah. Therefore, the following chapter will return to his theories in several instances.

The Kabbalah is also studied and practiced in groups, one of many qualities that demonstrates its close relationship to Jewish tradition, which has perpetuated collective study and interpretation of sacred texts for hundreds of years. It was Isaac Luria who recognized that in a group setting, each individual can experience spiritual enrichment through intensive examination of a Kabbalistic topic.

The development of theoretical Kabbalah after Luria

Over the course of the sixteenth century—not least due to the influence of Isaac Luria—the Kabbalah was studied openly and in groups for the first time in its history. From that time on, Kabbalists no longer studied in isolation, as they had until then, but with one another. In this way, each scholar's thinking was constantly exposed to new suggestions and developments. Thus, the study of the most important Kabbalistic texts continued to spread for another 200 years. During the Hasidic period—from around the middle of the eighteenth to the end of the nineteenth century—there were numerous Kabbalists in Poland and Russia, as well as in Morocco, Iraq, and Yemen; however, in Western Europe, interest in the theoretical Kabbalah decreased significantly until the end of the twentieth century, to the extent that it almost disappeared completely. Conversely, practical Kabbalah—which is

Today, there are Kabbalah centers in every Western country—for example, here in the United States. Pupils need not necessarily have knowledge of Hebrew in order to participate in the courses offered.

primarily concerned with sorcery using amulets and numerology, summoning geniuses (helpful spirits), and appealing to God through supernatural beings—became increasingly popular. It took another reformer of the theoretical Kabbalah to reignite people's interest in mystical thought structures and fundamental questions about the relationship between God and the world.

Rabbi Yehuda Ashlag, the Ba'al Ha-Sulam

Rabbi Yehuda Ashlag (1884–1956), called Ba'al Ha-Sulam, contributed additional teachings to those of Isaac Luria, thereby ushering in a third period in the development of the Kabbalah. Rabbi Ashlag also wrote a seminal commentary to the Zohar, called *Sulam*, or "ladder" as well as on the teachings of the Ari. Born in the Polish city of Lodz, Rabbi Yehuda Ashlag first worked as a judge and teacher in Warsaw. In 1921, he immigrated to Israel with his family and became a rabbi in Jerusalem. He began writing his commentary on the Zohar in 1943, finally completing it ten years later. His oldest

son, Rabbi Baruch Shalom Ashlag (1907–1991), called the Rabash, became his disciple and elaborated on his father's writings after his death, thus facilitating the study of these texts for many Kabbalists who followed.

A technique for advancing into the higher worlds

The Ba'al Ha-Sulam is the only Kabbalist of his generation to compose a comprehensive and up-to-date commentary on the Zohar and the writings of the Ari. The teaching method which his son illuminated is accessible for anyone who wishes to deepen their knowledge of the Kabbalah. All who devote themselves to its study are assured that within three to five years they will be capable of reaching spiritual spheres, recognizing true realities, and achieving a level of understanding approaching that of the Creator. Today, courses are offered in many countries that familiarize pupils with the practical and theoretical instructions of the Ba'al Ha-Sulam; corresponding audio CDs are even available, as well.

Kabbalists believe there are three aspects of the human soul, corresponding to the main groups of the Sefirot: rationality, sensation, and connection to nature.

THE KABBALISTIC IDEA OF MANKIND

In addition to understanding the nature of God, Kabbalists focus above all on questions of psychology and ethics. In their view, the human soul has three aspects: 1. *neshamah*—the soul endowed with reason, 2. *ruach*—the soul of sensation, and 3. *nephesh*—the vegetative soul, that is, the aspect that controls the functions of the body. All three of these Hebrew nouns are feminine, and they correspond to the three main groups of the ten Sefirot: the realm of reason, the realm of the soul, and the realm of nature (see p. 40f.)

The reasonable or rational area of the soul clearly reveals its divine origins. According to Kabbalists, every soul yearns to return to its source—that is, to God— and is thus able to advance to the higher realms. Nevertheless, the soul can also choose to turn to evil. The Kabbalah sees this as sinful, however, since it assumes that at its core, the soul consists of energy that strives in a morally upward direction, i.e. toward goodness, toward God.

Real preexistence

The Kabbalah believes that the soul is not created at the moment of conception, rather it already existed beforehand. It is located in a part of heaven where many souls are already waiting to take on a physical existence for the first time; others have returned to await rebirth. They take on an earthly existence to achieve perfection, but also in order to complete God's creation. A person who is not purified in one life will be born again. However, some Kabbalists do not rule out the possibility of incarnation in the body of an animal. Isaac Luria is said to have been able to recognize whether a person's soul was traveling through the world for the first time or on a repeated journey.

The necessity of transmigration

The Kabbalist Menasseh ben Israel (1604–1657), who was born in Lisbon and taught in Amsterdam as a preacher and rabbi, wrote a book entitled *Nishmat Hayim* ("Living Soul"). In it he points out, first of all, that "good and righteous people constantly experience misfortune, whereas bad people enjoy untarnished happiness, even though the opposite should rightfully

be true." Secondly, "children are often afflicted with the most terrible infirmities from birth on; indeed, they come into the world as unfortunate monsters, seemingly contradicting God's all-encompassing benevolence, from which, by definition, only good should come"; and thirdly, "children die very young, before they could possibly have sinned in their earthly existence, in apparent contradiction to God's mercifulness."

The Kabbalist's conclusions

From this, Menasseh ben Israel concluded that the righteous people who are currently suffering are atoning for wrongs committed in an earlier life. Therefore, the Kabbalist reasoned, these souls will also be better off in their next existence. Consequently, the evil people who are now living happily are the ones who were good in a previous earthly existence. In the mistaken belief that they will now be rewarded, they behave all the more badly—with the result that their next existence will be full of suffering. People who are born with deformities, said Menasseh ben Israel, have sinned grievously in their previous life, while children who die early must have abandoned themselves to evil in an earlier life and as punishment, are not allowed to remain in a single physical existence for long. Rather, they are transplanted into various bodies through early death and rebirth. Only perfect souls can enter the Hereafter; therefore, life on earth exists to purify us from sin—usually over the course of several lifetimes!

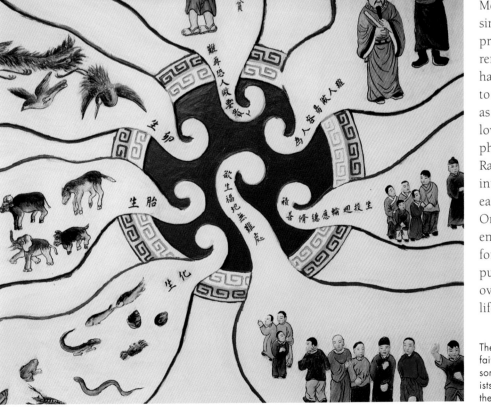

The cycle of rebirth in the Buddhist faith is similar to the beliefs held by some Kabbalists. There are Kabbalists who assume it is possible for the human soul to be reborn.

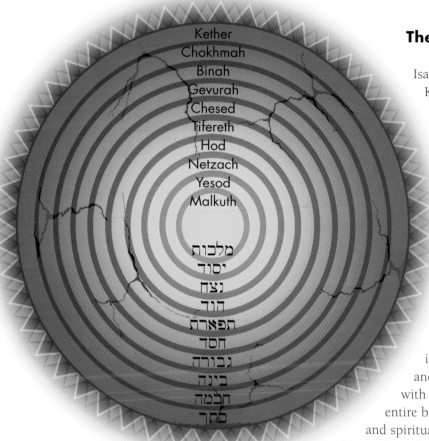

Kether
Chokhmah
Binah
Gevurah
Chesed
Tifereth
Hod
Netzach
Yesod
Malkuth

מלכות
יסוד
נצח
הוד
תפארת
חסד
גבורה
בינה
חכמה
כתר

Isaac Luria demonstrated the spherical configuration of the ten Sefirot according to the geocentric cosmology of his time—with the earth as the center of the universe. This depiction of the Lurianic model also integrates the "shattering of the vessels" (see p. 46).

The Lurianic spherical model

Isaac Luria seized upon the idea of Adam Kadmon and developed it further. In doing so, he formulated a spherical model of the first divine human, in which he linked the different parts of the soul. In the outermost stratum is "nephesh"—life energy or the vegetative soul; further inside lies "ruach"—the soul of sensation or the mind; and finally "neshama"—the rational soul or the spirit. In the center we find "ot"—the essence of all life—whose own central point is "yechida," or unity. This is the closest point to the divine source. In this model, the individual parts of the soul affect one another and are simultaneously connected with God. All of God's energies act upon the entire body. Adam Kadmon is the intellectual and spiritual prototype of the earthly human being: the radiant sparks of the Sefirot emanate from his eyes, ears and mouth.

Adam Kadmon, the "primordial man"

The story of Adam and Eve is also well-known in Christian cultural circles. Early Kabbalists paid special attention to the role of Adam in this story, whom they identified as the "primordial man," though this term has nothing in common with our modern concept of primitive human beings (in the sense of homo sapiens). According to the Kabbalah, Adam Kadmon was the first person God created in the Garden of Eden. But he is not to be confused with the first earthly human being: this man is called Adam HaRishon. Adam Kadmon is the first, the highest, divine, and cosmic man. He encompasses all of the ten Sefirot and can thus be depicted in the form of a tree. The divine Adam Kadmon is female as well as male—like the ten Sefirot. At the same time, he is the raw material for all of Creation, because the Sefirot also comprise this as a whole.

Adam Kadmon is the ideal image of a human being. The Creator modeled the world after him, as a reflection of the ten Sefirot.

The Golem

The Austrian author Gustav Meyrink (1868–1932), who converted from Protestantism to Mahayana Buddhism at the age of 59, also dealt with Kabbalistic tradition in his novels, and in 1915, his world-famous novel *The Golem* was published. Its title character is based on Rabbi Loew (pre-1525–1609), a Kabbalist from Prague who is said to have created the golem. Rabbi Loew, in turn, based his golem on the idea of Adam Kadmon. The term "golem" (lump) has been used in Jewish mysticism since time immemorial, denoting the lowest stratum of human existence. Before God breathed the power of life—neshamah– into Adam's body, he was a golem, a being created from the clay and dust of the earth. According to legend, Rabbi Loew first built his golem out of clay and then, in keeping with Kabbalistic belief, pasted a small sign under its tongue on which the word "shem" was written. After all, only God himself can blow neshamah, the energy of life, into a body. However, since the word "shem"—which means name—is also contained in "neshamah," Rabbi Loew believed that his golem would be imbued with the power of life as soon as he had discovered the true name of God.

The legend of the creation of the golem

On March 17, 1580, three men made their way to a clay pit on the Vltava River. Out of the heavy, wet clay, they fashioned a powerful figure with human features. Rabbi Loew then ordered his pupil to circle the golem seven times while reciting a Kabbalistic formula. The clay figure began to glow, and after the pupil had circled the golem seven times, the body became moist and began to emit steam; the golem grew hair and fingernails. Finally, Rabbi Loew recited a verse from Genesis (2:7): "And the LORD God ... breathed into his nostrils the breath of life; and man became a living soul." Thereupon the golem opened its eyes.

The story of the golem (shown here in a scene from the 1936 film of the same name), who having been created out of clay as God created the first man received the breath of life through the Word, is based on a Kabbalistic idea: God creates through the Word, and human beings imitate his actions.

THE DOCTRINE OF THE TREE OF LIFE

The Book of Genesis 2:9 tells us that there were two trees in Paradise: the Tree of Knowledge and the Tree of Life. The Tree of Knowledge produced the apple that gave human beings the awareness of good and evil—but they were forbidden to eat of it. When Adam and Eve defied God's order and ate the apple, they were banished from Paradise. From time immemorial, Kabbalists have also pondered the other tree, the Tree of Life, which they understand as the prototype for the ten Sefirot. God did not expressly forbid human beings from eating of the fruit of this tree, but what, the theoretical Kabbalah asks, is the significance of this tree?

The structure of the universe

The ten Sefirot are seen as the supporting pillars in the construction of the universe. In addition to the ten Sefirot, the radiant emanations of God, there are 22 energy paths that connect the individual Sefirot to one another. These paths not only correspond to the number of letters in the Hebrew alphabet, but also to the number of trumps in the Tarot. The Tree of Life illustrates how God descends in a ray of light from Kether—the crown—and travels through all the other Sefirot down to Malkuth, the earthly realm and ground level. In order to reach God, the soul must embark on a journey in the opposite direction. According to the Kabbalah, this is a long and laborious undertaking, during which a person must be prepared to face many setbacks, because the crucial factor in their success in scaling the Tree of Life from bottom to top is a pure soul. Such spiritual purity is only possible in the first place because the soul has its origins in God. In this sense, the human being is not only a reflection of the universe, but of God himself.

The Kabbalist notion of the ascent of the soul

The soul, which is trapped in the physical body, yearns to return to God: this is the primary assertion of the Kabbalah. The soul wants to reunite itself with its origins, and this is only possible when the body dies. Each Sefira, however, is guarded by angels who place obstacles in the soul's path. This, the Kabbalah explains, is due to the angels' fundamental jealousy toward human souls. The soul's ascent is most difficult at the beginning, at the lower end of the Tree of Life, since this is where the less benevolent angels (demons) reside. The higher the soul ascends, the kinder and more benevolent the angelic beings become. A soul can only prevail against the angels if, in the course of its earthly life, it has acquired sufficient knowledge about the secrets of each individual realm of the Sefirot. This, then, is where study of the Kabbalah can be put to practical use in the afterlife. The secret knowledge must also be attained through leading a pious life, as free as possible from sin.

The Kabbalah and magic

There is another means of ascending to the crown of the Tree of Life that can only be embarked upon as a person approaches death. This method employs a series of spiritual techniques in which the Kabbalah also instructs its followers. This is the point at which the practical Kabbalah, with its magical techniques, comes into play. Secret societies such as the Order of the Golden Dawn and mystics or occultists such as Aleister Crowley (1875–1947) were particularly drawn to the applications of the Kabbalah in this area (see p. 76f). Crowley, for example, learned to detach himself from the physical world in order to take a spiritual journey through the Sefirot. In order to do this, he needed to perfectly master the skills of concentration and visualization—for example, by means of a trance, a state of consciousness in which the psyche becomes detached from its day-to-day environment.

The ten Sefirot are connected by 22 energy paths; these correspond to the 22 letters of the Hebrew alphabet and are also known as "true paths." There are various models and interpretations of the mapping of the planets and colors. This illustration is based on the models of Carla Randel.

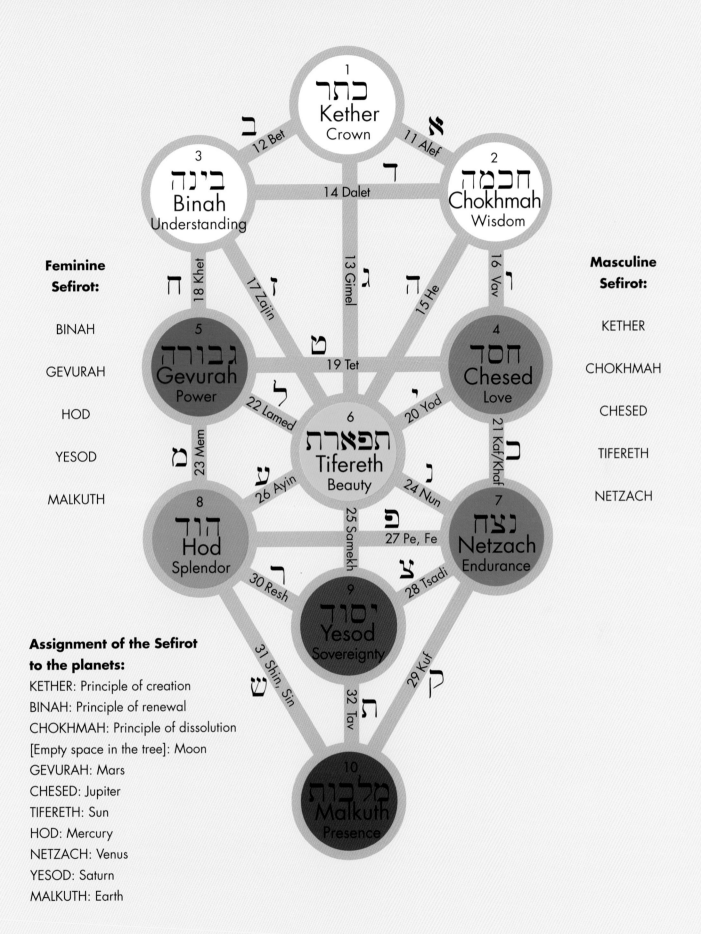

Feminine Sefirot:

BINAH

GEVURAH

HOD

YESOD

MALKUTH

Masculine Sefirot:

KETHER

CHOKHMAH

CHESED

TIFERETH

NETZACH

Assignment of the Sefirot to the planets:

KETHER: Principle of creation
BINAH: Principle of renewal
CHOKHMAH: Principle of dissolution
[Empty space in the tree]: Moon
GEVURAH: Mars
CHESED: Jupiter
TIFERETH: Sun
HOD: Mercury
NETZACH: Venus
YESOD: Saturn
MALKUTH: Earth

According to Isaac Luria, the divine light that represents the power of God was initially too strong for the world and needed to be filtered. This task fell to the ten Sefirot.

THE DOCTRINE OF TZIMTZUM

Isaac Luria's doctrine of Tzimtzum is one of the great Kabbalist's most controversial ideas; at the same time, it introduced a fascinating philosophical angle on the question of how evil entered the world. Kabbalists hold that God created the world out of nothingness. Early mystical theories of Judaism assumed that God created the world directly from himself, but the question as to why human beings think and behave in ways so unlike God remained unanswered.

What, then, is the origin of evil? How did evil come into the world? Luria provides an extraordinary answer: in the course of his Creation, God withdrew himself! God first created empty space in which to create the universe. He then sent out emanations of divine light, through which Creation was set in motion. This light was too strong for the world,

however, and thus the ten Sefirot became "interme-diaries." They filter the "light"—the power of God—and reduce its strength. Luria's doctrine of Tzimtzum says nothing more than this; the word itself means "contraction" or "constriction." Nevertheless, the question that remained in dispute among Kabbalists was whether evil was able to evolve because of the chaos that resulted when God withdrew from the world, or rather—as Chaim Vital suggests—through

"Thought-some" and "thought-less" light

According to Kabbalist Nathan of Gaza (1644–1680), two lights have burned within God since the dawn of time: "thought-some" light and "thought-less" light. The active and thought-filled light affirms Creation, while thought-less, passive light inhibits Creation through its indifference. Nathan of Gaza believed that the basis of all evil is this thought-less light within God himself, which rejects Creation. In the scenario he envisioned, the two aspects of God struggle against each other; the evil aspect is the part of God that would rather rest than create.

the very emptiness itself that was created when Ein Sof was contracted.

God's abdication

According to Luria's explanation, God did not wish that everything should be god-like. Therefore, he retreated from his creation, leaving it open to the various processes that influence the fate of the world. God created humans in his own image, but he did not impose his own choices upon them; thus, he left room for the struggle between good and evil. This interpretation is diametrically opposed to the traditional Christian notion, for example. In that view, evil also entered the world through mankind's free will; however, it had already existed in the form of the devil, who disguised himself as a serpent in Paradise. In every era, Kabbalists have debated about God's behavior in the act of

In Judaism as well as in Christianity, people are free to make their own choices. In this way, God places the responsibility for which path they will pursue—whether toward good or toward evil—in the hands of his creations.

Some Kabbalists believe that after creating Adam, God withdrew from the world, thereby making room for the struggle between good and evil.

Creation. The doctrine of the Tzimtzum opens the possibility for human beings to exert their free will in relationship to God. Nevertheless, even Kabbalists aspire to return to the original state of goodness. Whether or not individuals actively take part in this return, and the degree to which they contribute to the victory of goodness, is entirely up to them.

The nature of God

All Kabbalists seek the true name of God in order to better understand his nature. Luria and his pupils discovered numerous secret names. These are frequently combinations of the letters Yod, He, and Vav—which make up the Biblical first name of God, Yahweh. Thus, Luria's followers already considered the path to discovering God's true name to be an opportunity to become one with him. Luria himself advised all Kabbalists to keep any name they discovered secret and to write it on an amulet that they should then carry with them at all times in order to meditate on it and incorporate it into their prayers. In this sense, the Lurianic Kabbalah is concerned not only with discovering the nature of God, but also with human salvation.

THE DOCTRINE OF THE FOUR REALMS

The Kabbalistic doctrine of the four worlds tells us that God is constantly creating and maintaining the world as the four realms—Atzilut, Beri'ah, Yetzirah, and Asiyah—flow into and interact with one another.

Luria and his followers attempted to understand the way in which God takes an active part in his creation. In the process, they developed the doctrine of the "four worlds." Like other Kabbalistic concepts before it, the doctrine assumes that human beings are copies of God, and therefore, any attempt to understand God's actions must necessarily include observation of human behavior.

How, then, does God act? Similarly to human beings: God first makes a decision to do something, make something or create something. This is the first realm of emanation or radiance, called Atzilut. Next, God develops detailed ideas for the plan. Kabbalists call this second realm of Creation Beri'ah. The next step is the planning and gathering of raw material; this is the third realm of formation, called Yetzirah. Finally, there is the actual act of creation and the interaction of all of the elements. This realm of execution is called Asiyah. According to Kabbalistic understanding, all four worlds or realms exist simultaneously; thus, they do not describe a linear process, but rather the constant, unceasing workings of God.

God in constant action

The Kabbalist Yeshaya Horowitz (ca. 1560–1630) wrote: "When Ein Sof creates the Atzilut, the souls of everything in the universe are dispersed. This leads to Beri'ah (Creation), which leads to Yetzirah; Yetzirah then guides the Atzilut into Asiyah. All of this continues without interruption." What may seem complicated at first glance can easily be broken up into single steps. The second step follows from the first; the third follows from the second, and the fourth from the third. The concept that is crucial to Kabbalistic understanding is that this is not a single, non-recurring act of God, but rather a continuous process: God is constantly in action!

A summary of the four realms of the Kabbalah

1. Atzilut

Atzilut is the realm of the Sefirot or the first radiance (emanation) of the Ein Sof; Ein Sof is the unfathomable God, the Absolute.

2. Beri'ah

Beri'ah is the realm of Creation or of the ideas of the world, which—like the Sefirot—are conceived of in groups of ten. Some Kabbalists also call this the "world of angels."

According to Luria's teachings, Asiyah—the material world in which human beings live—is just one of the four worlds created by God.

3. Yetzirah

Yetzirah is the realm of Formation, which, in turn, is intended as the prototype for material existence. Some Kabbalists also call Yetzirah the "realm of souls."

4. Asiyah

Finally, Asiyah is the realm of Actions or occurrences, the material world in which human beings live.

All four of these worlds interact with one another. Everything that exists below—in the world of Actions—owes its appearance to the higher world, where it has its prototype. This interrelationship is what makes it possible to elevate oneself and evolve spiritually from the lower region into the one above.

TIKKUN: THE HEALING

Creation will be completed when the primordial state, as God intended it, is restored. The Kabbalah describes how this can be accomplished—the way in which a human being can heal him or herself and thus gradually perfect the material world. Tikkun is healing—and it takes effect as soon as a person attempts to come close to God through Kabbalistic action. The simple attempt to put the broken vessels of the Sefirot—the "qlippoth"—back together sets the healing process in motion. The Kabbalah enumerates the three areas, separated by God, which need to experience Tikkun: the self, the world, and the presence of God in the world. In ancient times, before Creation began, these three things were united within Ein Sof. In his book, *The Two Tables of the Covenant*, Yeshayah Horowitz described the Creation as a catastrophe, an accident that tore the three previously united areas apart.

The breaking of the vessels

When Ein Sof contracted at the beginning of Creation, in order to make room for the universe, he placed vessels filled with divine light in the resulting empty space. The three uppermost "Sefirot vessels" preserved the light, but the seven lower Sefirot vessels shattered. The result was the imperfect "qlippoth"—shards that are seen as the cause of evil. Every soul must now attempt to glue the shards back together, because human beings are made up of these shards and of divine light. Therefore, according to the Kabbalah, human beings are not bad, they are simply imperfect. When enough souls have "purified" themselves—when the vessels have been repaired—the universe can be perfected. At the same time, Tikkun—the restoration of the original state—will be completed.

The Kabbalistic concept of the "breaking of the vessels," through which the world was rendered imperfect, provides a vivid picture of why Creation is not perfect and all human beings are not only good.

THE CONCEPT OF RITUAL PURITY

According to Kabbalism, music can cleanse the soul from pollution. The light-hearted yet melancholy sound of klezmer music—here, scene from a klezmer festival in New York—is thought to release purifying energy.

In addition to meditation on the ten Sefirot, the Lurianic Kabbalah also includes the ancient Jewish concept of ritual purity. Since the earliest times, washing oneself before prayer has been customary in Judaism. Luria required his followers to begin the day by immersing themselves in the mikvah, the Jewish ritual bath used for purification. As symbols of their purity, Luria and his disciples wore simple white caps and stoles. Ritual purity provides a signal to evil forces that there is no place for them in this body and this soul. The daily service of God is focused on the search for wisdom, on prayer, and on meditation on the Sefirot.

Pleasure and joy are part of the Kabbalah

Kabbalists do not castigate themselves. They are not concerned with asceticism and punishment. The Ari himself repeatedly emphasized the enjoyment of music and dance. Here, Kabbalists point to the 100th Psalm,

which says: "Serve the LORD with gladness: come before his presence with singing." Isaac Luria said that every religious action and every meditation on God and his creation should be carried out with enthusiasm. At the same time, music can cleanse the soul and free it from the "grime" of everyday life.

The mikvah

The Jewish ritual immersion bath is called a mikvah. In earlier centuries, one of these small baths could be found in nearly every Jewish community. Even today, the construction and usage of a mikvah are subject to a number of rules: it is essential that the water be flowing, natural water; therefore, only spring water, ground water or collected rainwater is acceptable. Nowadays, mikvahs resemble modern bathing facilities. Anyone entering a mikvah should be completely naked; even lipstick and nail polish are forbidden. The bather must immerse their entire body, including the hair. Traditional Jewish laws prescribe visits to the mikvah for both men and women. Men are instructed to immerse themselves before the Sabbath or before the Day of Atonement, Yom Kippur. Women should visit the mikvah on the evening before they are married, following menstruation or after the birth of a child. To this day, immersion in the mikvah is also required of scribes of the Torah before they begin their work.

The ruins of a historic mikvah in Masada, Israel.

ANGELS, CREATURES OF DIVINE LIGHT

Scripture indicates that angels existed even before the formation of the world; however, the actual realm of angels is not described in further detail. For all intents and purposes, Christianity only recognizes two individual angels—Michael and Gabriel—who appear in the role of messengers as well as destroyers. Judaism recognizes a great many more angels, and the Christian religion adopted the concept of angels from Judaism, including that of their hierarchies. The Books of Moses mention angelic guards in Paradise; angels destroyed the city of Sodom, and an angel informed Mary that she was expecting a child. The wings with which angels are usually depicted symbolize their closeness to God and their ability to ascend above the level of humankind. The fallen angel Satan (or Lucifer) was originally reputed to be an especially beautiful angel, but one who turned against God. His task is to tempt people and lead them away from the right path.

Angels in Judaism

Judaism speaks of four Archangels: Gabriel, the angel of fire and war; Uriel, the angel of divine light; Raphael, the angel of healing; and Michael, the angel of mercy. The four Archangels accompany good people at their birth.

According to the Zohar, God created these and all other good angels out of divine light on the very first day of Creation. On the second day, the Zohar says, God created the less benevolent angels out of fire. However, all the hosts of angels act according to the will of God.

In addition to the four Archangels, Judaism also recognizes another important angel: Metatron. He accompanies those people who meditate on the world and its phenomena. In Judaism, angels represent the choices and opportunities available to a person.

God's less benevolent angels

An idea that is unthinkable in Christianity—namely that God could also have created angels who were less than good—is, for Kabbalists, an aspect of divine Creation. The Zohar says that the birth of a person whose family tree contains nothing good will be accompanied by the four forces of evil: rage,

God created Satan and the other evil angels out of fire. According to Kabbalistic understanding, the "dark" powers of the universe are as much a part of Creation as the "light" ones.

In this fifteenth-century painting by Filipino Lippi, three Archangels accompany a boy named Tobias; they carry a lily, a sword and a messenger's staff to help them ward off the devil. In contrast to Christianity, Judaism and the Kabbalah recognize a fourth Archangel: Uriel, the angel of divine light.

destruction, depravity, and impatience. Beneath the Archangels are a multitude of lower angels who are responsible for specific things, like animals and plants, or such abstract processes as seconds, minutes, hours, and days. Below this stratum, in turn, reside the less benevolent angels. The Kabbalah specifically states that they are not evil in and of themselves; rather, that they simply introduce negative energies into the world. Human beings must resist these negative powers and their temptations—this is the very reason that these angels exist. Unlike in Christianity, Satan is not perceived as the primary evil-doer, but rather as an "obstacle." Another of these evil angels is Lilith, who by night seduces men and kills children. According to Jewish lore, Lilith was also the first wife of Adam; but Lilith was so headstrong that Adam complained to God and asked him to provide him with a more compliant wife.

PRAYER AND MEDITATION

Every prayer is an attempt on the part of a person to make contact with the Supreme Being to whom he or she prays—a dialogue that may range from obeisant humility to a request. The early Jewish Kabbalists saw prayer as simply a supplementary action: to them, observance of the commandments and contemplation of the ten Sefirot were much more important.

Over the centuries, though, the significance of prayer in the Kabbalah changed. For the Spanish mystics, preparations for prayer, for dialogue with God, became a particularly important exercise in concentration, which they called "kavanot." These kavanot included strongly meditative elements; practitioners generally used Biblical Psalms for this purpose. Since Kabbalists are always searching for the true name of God, they created new names for God using the first letters of a given Psalm—using a procedure similar to that used for creation of the 72 angels' names (see p. 69). In the Zohar, we find evidence that the kavanot represent means of allowing the soul to ascend to heaven. In this way, Kabbalist mystics hoped to experience the true presence of God in their hearts. The Zohar says that an angel descends during evening prayers and carries the most fervent prayer up to heaven on its wings.

Kabbalists traditionally consider spontaneous prayer to be more significant than collective prayers in the synagogue.

Whereas early Kabbalists considered prayer to be simply a supplement to religious life, it has much greater significance today.

Kabbalistic meditation on "amen"

The origin and meaning of the word "amen," which is used by Jews and Christians alike, are shrouded in mystery. In the Christian context, it is generally translated as "so be it!" Since the most ancient times, however, Kabbalists have used the word "amen" to express a beseeching request, an appeal to God. The three Hebrew letters that make up the word are Alef, Mem, and Nun. These are also the initial letters in three Hebrew words that are closely associated with God, namely *adonai*—Lord, *melekh*—king, and *ne'eman*—trustworthy. Thus, in its Kabbalistic interpretation, "amen" takes on an appellative character—"Lord, trusted king!"—and provides more extensive grounds for meditating on the word "amen." While this can no doubt take place in a synagogue, the spiritual thoughts of the Kabbalah are not bound to a particular holy place.

After the Jews were driven out of the Holy Land by the Roman emperor Titus in the year 70, the first synagogues were built outside of that region. This synagogue in Prague—known as Staronova—is thought to be the oldest in Europe.

The synagogue

The Jewish house of worship serves both as a gathering place and as a place of instruction for the faithful. The term "synagogue" is derived from a Greek word meaning "the community that gathers together." The Hebrew term *beit knesset* has exactly the same meaning. The first synagogues were built after the Temple in Jerusalem was destroyed by the Romans. A synagogue always faces toward Jerusalem. The development of architectural style in synagogue construction was always influenced by contemporary forms, with the result that there is no one typical building style. Only the interior always features the same objects used in ritual practice: a replica of the menorah (the seven-armed candelabrum used in the temple), a Torah shrine, a pulpit and a Chanukkiyah—a Chanukka candelabrum (Chanukka is the eight-day-long festival of lights in the middle of December that commemorates the rededication of the Temple in Jerusalem in the year 164 BC).

Two types of prayer

There are two types of Jewish prayer, those spoken in the synagogue in the context of a service, and spontaneous prayer uttered during everyday life. Kabbalists consider the latter to be the more valuable. Prayers can heal people—although it is particularly spiritual health that is meant here. Prayers can influence angels and even reach God, if a person can discover his true name. A person who is able to pray using God's true name is a "Ba'al Shem Tov"—a "master of the divine name."

PRACTICAL
KABBALAH

ESTABLISHING CORRELATIONS

No aspect of human existence is foreign to the Kabbalah. Along with speculations about God and his Creation as well as the search for his true name; along with prayer, meditation, and the ascent of the soul into higher worlds; the Kabbalah also encompasses astrological concepts as well as thoughts on sexuality and death. Magic is also one of the subjects of the Kabbalah, even if this is never expressly stated. Highly developed religions such as Judaism as well as Christianity tend to look at magic—such as that practiced in tribal religions, for example—as a form of superstition. To them, magic is a godless practice, or one which is opposed to God, since in practicing magic, a person presumes to do something which, according to their beliefs, he or she is not entitled to do—namely, to obtain and exercise control over things, animals or people using supernatural powers.

Because of its seven arms and (originally) three feet, Kabbalists see a connection between the menorah and the ten Sefirot.

The menorah

The menorah is the seven-armed candelabrum mentioned in the Book of Exodus as the central ritual object in the Jewish Temple in Jerusalem. In the Kabbalah it is a symbol of God's power, through which he can intervene in the fate of human beings. He repeatedly appeared to the Israelites in the guise of fire, for example: as the burning bush through which God spoke to Moses, or the pillar of fire that appeared during the Israelites' flight out of Egypt. Therefore, the menorah is a symbol that constantly reappears in Kabbalistic texts, often serving Kabbalists as an aide to concentration. In the practical Kabbalah, however, the menorah is also put to concrete use, for example, to invoke the 72 geniuses or angels. When the Roman emperor Titus captured Jerusalem and plundered the Temple treasury in the year 70 AD, he brought the original menorah back to Rome with him as a trophy of his victory. The Visigoth king Alaric I stole it again in the year 410. After this, all traces of it have been lost in the sands of time.

The Kabbalah never specifically refers to magical processes, even though it claims to set these very phenomena in motion. It also aims to banish or overcome dark forces—for example, by invoking the names of God or the angels. In addition, the Kabbalah employs certain objects and (magical) procedures for fending off evil.

Analogies between the worlds

The effectiveness of magic is based on the assumption of analogies between the visible and invisible worlds. The legendary figure Hermes Trismegistos (Greek: "Hermes the Thrice-Great") is considered to be the first magician to formulate this correlation. He is a compilation of at least two Mediterranean deities: Thoth, the Egyptian god of wisdom and magic, and Hermes, the Greek god and divine messenger who was responsible for such things as nature, messages, dreams, travelers' paths, commerce, and money. In the Tabula Smaragdina, or Emerald Tablet, a group of hermetic texts that were written in the second and third centuries—primarily in Greek, Latin and Coptic scripts—and attributed to Hermes Trismegistos, we read: "That which is below is like that which is above, and that which is above is like that which is below to do the miracles of one only thing."

Establishing correlations

Just like magic, the practical Kabbalah aims to establish correlations. From a Kabbalistic viewpoint, these correlations exist in the sense that everything a person thinks or does (be it positive or negative) has consequences on the spiritual as well as on the material level. In this way, everything is connected with everything else: the tree of the ten Sefirot and the 22 paths illustrate exactly this concept. And just like magic, the practical Kabbalah refers to the analogy model formulated by Hermes Trismegistos: that which is below (the earth) is the same as that which is above (heaven), and those who recognizes this can perform miracles— that is, they can practice magic. The Book of Genesis says that God created human beings in his own image. From this, Kabbalists deduce that human beings are connected to the cosmos, from which they can obtain the power to influence objects, situations, and people within their earthly existence.

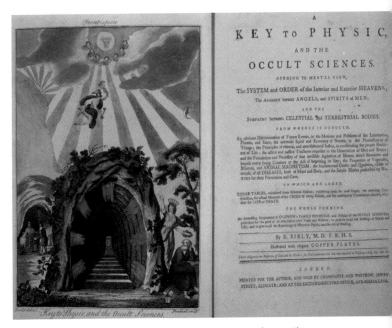

Hermes Trismegistos is the god of occultism and its sacred texts. The term "hermetic" literature—among which we can also count the Kabbalah—is derived from his name.

THE POWER OF AMULETS

A talisman in the form of a good luck charm that contains a piece of text from the Talmud. The boxer Barney Ross is said to have partially attributed his winning of the 1934 welterweight title to this talisman.

In addition to polished gemstones—if not as frequently—practical Kabbalists use engraved amulets, in which a protective formula or figure is carved on a piece of metal or glass or on a precious stone. Also common are parchment or leather amulets inscribed with the various names of God, or the angels or with words of blessing from the scriptures. In order to ward off the demon Lilith, who is said to kill small children, the Kabbalah advises hanging an amulet bearing one of the names of God on the bed of a woman giving birth. The phrase inscribed on it may be, for example, "Adam, Eve—out, Lilith!" Naturally, the amulet must be engraved with Hebrew letters. Frequently, a six-pointed Star of David also appears as an additional protective symbol.

Amulets and talismans

Both amulets and talismans have a long history; there is hardly a race of people on earth that does not know or make use of them. Talismans are generally material objects to which some magical, invisible power has been ascribed that cannot be physically proven. They are intended to help their owner in a specific desired way. Amulets have a primarily protective function, whereas talismans are more like good luck charms. Amulets and talismans are frequently made out of neutral brass or copper. According to their wearers, this material serves to absorb any harmful or unfavorable energy and draw it away from the body. An amulet should only ever serve one person, who, by cleaning it, endows the object with his or her own personal qualities. A modern variation on the talisman is a mascot.

"Chamsa"—the hand—is an amulet used to protect against the evil eye. Amulets such as this were, and are, used by Kabbalists. This and other amulets were discovered in Safed, once the center of Kabbalah.

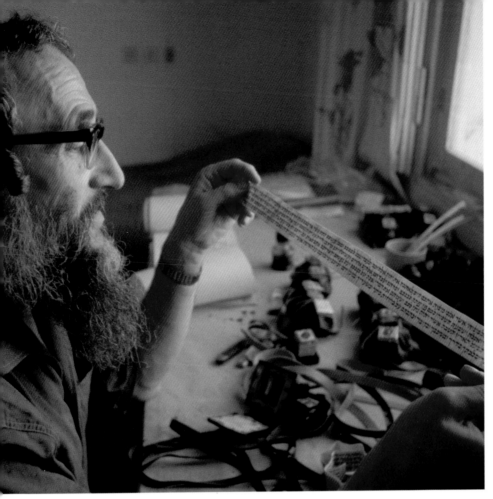

Astrological talismans

Due to their allocation to the individual planets—each of which, in turn, is related to one of the Sefirot—various gemstones and metals can be used as astrological talismans. Here, a person may employ one of the following seven gemstones: carbuncle, crystal, diamond, emerald, agate, sapphire or onyx. Likewise, one of the following seven metals may be used: gold, silver, iron, copper, mercury, tin or lead. Sometimes they are also attributed to one of the seven angels, who serve as protectors.

Holy words from the Torah or Kabbalistic texts written on strips of paper are thought to protect people from evil and adversity. Such use of powerful words has been practiced in every era of the Kabbalah.

Kamea: magic number squares

Some engraved amulets feature magic number squares, in which the sum of the numbers in every direction—horizontally, vertically, and diagonally—yields the same result. These magical number squares are associated with metals and with the seven earliest known planets (Mars, Jupiter, the Sun, Mercury, Saturn, Venus, and Earth), whereby each metal is attributed to a particular planet. A Kamea offers protection to the person who uses it in relation to the planet or planets found in the first house of his or her birth horoscope. There are a total of seven magical number squares, which in turn are correlated with the seven lower Sefirot (Malkuth, Yesod, Hod, Netzach, Tifereth, Gevurah, and Chesed). Out of reverence for the divine sphere, the three highest Sefirot (Kether, Binah, Chokhmah) are not included. One example of such a magical number square is the 3 x 3 "Kamea of Lead." In addition, there is a 4 x 4 square, a 5 x 5 square, and so forth—up until the last Kamea, the 9 x 9 square.

The Kamea of Lead—whose horizontal, vertical and diagonal sums all add up to the number 15, and which corresponds to the Sefira Malkuth—is composed as follows:

4	9	2
3	5	7
8	1	6

KABBALISTIC ASTROLOGY

Even though the Zohar rejects astrology, calling it a "mendacious science," some Kabbalists have nevertheless made intense study of the "wisdom of the stars." In the middle of the twelfth century, in particular, many rabbis served as court astrologers for the Castilian kings. One important Kabbalistic astrologer was Abraham ibn Ezra (1192–1167) from northern Spain; another scholar, Abraham Zacuto (1460–1510), wrote the book *Sefer Hayuhasin*—the book of genealogies—and was a respected astrologer at the court of King Manuel of Portugal. The most important astrological and alchemistic work written by a medieval Kabbalist is the *Aesch Mezareph*—the Purifying Fire. Its author is unknown; however, it is assumed to be the work of an Italian Kabbalist from the early sixteenth century.

The power of the seven planets

The number seven has been considered especially significant throughout the history of Judaism. Above and beyond this, in the Kabbalah, it symbolizes the entire power of the universe: seven planets, seven days

In the Middle Ages, astrology was considered to be highly significant. This is due to the fact that at that time, people still thought of themselves as very much a part of nature and the cosmos.

In antiquity, only seven of the planets in our solar system were known: the sun and moon were counted among them, along with Mercury, Venus, Mars, Jupiter, and Saturn.

Correlations of the planets

One hallmark of Kabbalistic astrology is the connection of the planets to the ten Sefirot. In the *Aesch Mezareph* (the Purifying Fire) the ten Sefirot are correlated with the individual planets as follows: Chokhmah—Saturn; Binah and Netzach—Jupiter; Gevurah—the Sun; Tifereth—Mars; Chesed—the Moon; Hod—Venus; Yesod—Mercury. Other exponents of astrological Kabbalah, however, classify the planets differently: Gevurah—Mars; Tifereth—the Sun; Chesed—Jupiter; Hod—Mercury; Yesod—Saturn; Netzach—Venus; Malkuth—Earth. This system is remarkable for the fact that no planets are attributed to the three highest Sefirot. These are instead associated with three principles of Creation—namely formation, renewal, and dissolution. The moon, however, is assigned to the empty space between the upper realm, Atzilut and the realm of Beri'ah. In contrast to classical astrology, in which the future is predicted based on the positions of the planets, Kabbalistic astrology focuses on people's behavior. Since we are endowed with free will, we can overcome the influence of the stars if we concentrate completely on the divine energies. At the same time, the Kabbalah assumes that God guides the planets' paths. Thus, for astrological Kabbalists, the "wisdom of the stars" provides us with a means of understanding people's thoughts and behavior; it is not concerned with predicting the future.

of the week, the seven arms of the menorah, the seven lower Sefirot, the seven colors of the prism, the seven notes in music, etc. It plays a special role in Kabbalistic astrology, which presumes the existence of seven planets—Sun, Moon, Mars, Venus, Mercury, Jupiter, and Saturn—which it ascribes to the seven angels Michael, Gabriel, Samael, Aniel, Raphael, Zachariel, and Orifiel. These angels influence people throughout their entire lifetime.

Kabbalistic astrologers believe that each person's life is governed by predetermined developmental laws, which they attempt to interpret. Thus, they calculate the influence of a given angel based on the orbit of the planet with which that angel is associated. At the same time, they connect each planet with a particular stage of human life: the sun is associated with childhood; the moon with the developing child. Mars and Venus are related to male and female adolescence, respectively; the prime of male or female life is associated with Mercury and maturity with Jupiter. Finally, Saturn is the planet that governs old age.

The number seven symbolizes the power of the universe; it can be found, among other things, in the seven colors of the spectrum (red, orange, yellow, green, cyan, blue, violet). These are also called the colors of the rainbow, since they are the colors we can recognize in this phenomenon.

GEMATRIA: THE MAGIC OF NUMBERS

The idea that certain numbers possess special magical powers was already significant in early Judaism. According to Jewish tradition, for instance, when Joshua conquered the city of Jericho he is said to have ultimately used numerology to bring about the collapse of the city walls. The story tells us that he and his army besieged the city for seven days, surrounding it seven times during that period. He was accompanied by seven priests carrying seven trumpets. On the seventh day, the seven priests sounded their seven trumpets, and the walls fell down.

Hebrew numerology

Early in their history, Kabbalists developed a technique for the interpretation and permutation of Hebrew words and their respective numerical values; this method bears strong similarities to what is known as the Abjad system (an emblematic transcription of letter-numeral-letter), the mystical Islamic movement of the Sufis. The Kabbalistic method—called gematria—was later adopted by other cultures as well, including the Greeks and Romans.

An anecdote from ancient Greece tells of an anonymous poet who wished to use gematria to prove that his arch rival, the poet Damagoras, was more evil than the plague. A numerical interpretation of the name Damagoras results in a value of 425. The plague (Greek: "loimos"), on the other hand, has a numerical value of only 410. What might cause a matter-of-fact modern reader to merely smile is highly significant to a Kabbalist. For Kabbalists, the numbers never lie. After all, they are based on the Hebrew letters, whose origins are divine.

The legacy of the Pythagoreans

The question of whether Pythagoras (approx. 570–500 BC) adopted his numerical teachings from Jewish scholars, or whether the reverse is true, continues to be a matter of debate to this day. His pupils developed numerous ideas which remained alive in later numerical mysticism (the Pythagoreans already saw numbers as the guarantors of universal harmony), and the two systems certainly contain many similarities. Both, for example, show a preference for odd numbers, which stood out from the even numbers because they were associated with masculinity, restfulness, light, and goodness (the right side of the Sefirot). The even numbers, on the other hand—because they are

The Greek philosopher Pythagoras discovered the fundamental principles of world events in numbers and numerical relationships. The contrast between even and odd numbers, for example, is reflected throughout the entire Cosmos.

Kabbalistic practice took effect at the collapse of the walls of Jericho. Not only the sounding of the mighty trumpets, but the power of the numbers themselves proved their tremendous effectiveness.

endlessly divisible—were associated with that which is limitless, feminine, emotional, dark, and evil (the left side of the Sefirot). In magic as well as in the Kabbalah, odd numbers are dominant and have greater significance. Magical knots are tied an odd number of times, for example, and magical practices are carried out among groups consisting of an odd number of people.

Gnosis and the Kabbalah

Gnosis—the doctrine of the revelation or knowledge of cosmic secrets through the soul—also made use of Kabbalistic numerology, endowing every number with a metaphysical significance that may be summed up in three statements:

1. A number influences the nature of the things which are ordered within it, in whatever way that may be.

2. In this way, the number becomes an intermediary between the divine and the earthly spheres.

3. Magical or Kabbalistic procedures that are carried out using numbers influence the aforementioned objects because of their association with those numbers.

According to the numerical mystics of every culture that practices the art of gematria, anyone who separates the numbers from the objects (which is, in fact, impossible) will destroy the universe.

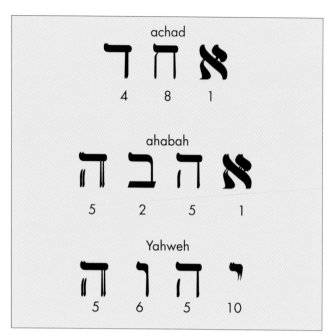

achad

אחד
4 8 1

ahabah

אהבה
5 2 5 1

Yahweh

יהוה
5 6 5 10

Addition is an important factor in gematria. The individual values of the letters in a word are added together to reveal their implicit messages.

The magic of ten

In Jewish mysticism—at its core no different than in Pythagorean thought—the number ten has always played a central role. In addition to the ten Sefirot, Jewish tradition recognizes the Ten Commandments and counts ten generations leading to Noah; the Torah tells us ten times, "And God said," and Kabbalists believe God's throne rests on ten pillars. God sent ten plagues upon the Egyptians before his people finally gained their freedom. Ten represents a rounded whole, and at the same time refers back to one—the number that permeates every other and symbolizes the ancient One, God himself. Keeping in mind that each Hebrew letter also symbolizes a number, the letter "Alef" is identical to the number one. For this reason alone, the Kabbalist Rabbi Akiva (died ca. 135 AD) was able to write in his book *Otiyot*—The Alphabet—that before anything else existed, one letter after another appeared before God and said: "Create the world through me!"

In Jewish mysticism, numbers are not seen as units of measurement, but rather as a means for the divine to reveal itself. Among others, the number ten plays a central role and is reflected, for example, in the Ten Commandments.

A gematric example

As already stated, for Kabbalists, God is the "One," the single divine entity, the origin of everything. The Hebrew word for one is "achad," which is spelled as follows: Alef (1) + Khet (8) + Dalet (4). Adding the numerical values of the letters results in the number 13. The word "ahabah" means love, and is spelled Alef (1) + He (5) + Bet (2) + He (5). The sum of the values of these letters is, again, 13. Thus, Kabbalists conclude, love and oneness (God) are identical in nature. They also take the idea a step further: adding the two values (13+13) results in the numerical value of God's name, Yahweh—Yod (10), He (5), Vav (6) and He (5). In this way, Kabbalists are able to decipher even difficult verses in scripture and reveal their secret messages. In Genesis 49:10, for example, we find the Hebrew text *yabo shiyloh*—"until Shiloh come." No one knows what is meant by the name Shiloh. A Kabbalist schooled in gematria, however, can use the numerical values of the words "shiyloh" and "moshiach" (Messiah) to recognize that the nature of the two words is the same. This allows the mysterious word "Shiloh," and thus the entire sentence, to take on a meaning.

Gematria,
a dialogue with the Most High

In the names of God that are known to Kabbalists, the letters that occur most frequently are He (5) and Yod (10). The ten Sefirot can be divided into two groups of five each, five masculine Sefirot and five feminine Sefirot. Thus, with the aid of the most common names of God and the letters they most often contain—along with their numbers, 5 and 10—Kabbalists can discover, so to speak, a built-in confirmation that the Sefirot are connected with God. Furthermore, of the ten Sefirot, seven are associated with the body (those in the lower strata) and three (in the upper strata) with the mind. With the help of these two numbers—3 and 7—then, a dialogue with God can take place.

The origin of the Tarot cards (shown here, a French deck) is unknown to this day. The fact that we refer to 22 of them as trump cards—also called the major arcana—is, to Kabbalists, an indication that a hidden relationship exists between the Tarot and the Hebrew alphabet.

The number 22 and the Tarot

The 22 Hebrew letters are also associated with the 22 trump cards of the Tarot (the major arcana)—the "allegories" that relate to basic human situations. The oldest known Tarot cards originated in Italy in the year 1465, and the pictures on that deck exhibit references to Egyptian and Kabbalistic mysticism. The first Kabbalist to recognize this was Eliphas Levi (1810–1875), and his work, *The Dogma and Ritual of High Magic*, deals with the secret connections between numbers, the Tarot, and letters. His teachings also influenced Kabbalistic astrology. By adding the digits (letters) of each name and then adding those sums, he transformed any given person's first and last names into a number; to this he added the cross sum of the person's birth date. The resulting "fateful number" was the highly influential basis for producing a horoscope.

Mystical gematria and rational world views

The fact that mystical gematria and a rational understanding of the world are not necessarily contradictory ideas may be illustrated by the following historical example. The numerical value of the Hebrew word "makhom" (which means space or place) can be calculated according to the method explained above. When we add the numerical values of the individual Hebrew letters, the resulting sum is 186. If we then take the numerical values of each of the four Hebrew letters in the Tetragrammaton—YHWH (10, 5, 6, 5)—multiply each one by itself, and then add the resulting squared values together, the result is also 186. To a Kabbalist, this result confirms that God and space are the same thing. However, since God knows no limits—that is, God is infinite—Kabbalists were able to logically come to the conclusion that space, too, is without limits. Thus, the Kabbalah formulated the first concept of the universe as an infinite space, and as a result, influenced medieval scientific thought in a revolutionary way.

Reverse conclusions using the gematric Kabbalah

Kabbalists and numerologists have often attempted to attribute certain numbers to particular individuals. Some recent scholars have been especially fascinated by the "Number of the Beast"—666—mentioned in the Revelation of St. John the Divine (Revelation 13:18). According to the Book of Revelation, the number 666 refers to a certain concrete person. To St. John the Divine, the number 666 represented the Antichrist. This vague statement naturally has sparked the imaginations of many a numerologist. In earlier eras, the Roman emperor Nero and Martin Luther both came into consideration as candidates, since the letters of their names can be converted into exactly this number; however, the reverse process proved nearly impossible.

The Apocalyse as depicted by the painter and illustrator Albrecht Dürer (1471–1528). For hundreds of years, the Book of the Apocalypse (or Revelation) has evoked countless conspiracy theories and occult fantasies unlike any other text in history.

that is sold—are places in which Satan is hiding. Since every group of lines in a barcode stands for a number, they assume that each pair of thin lines represents the number six. However, the code is generally divided into sections using three longer pairs of lines; from this, modern numerologists conclude with absolute conviction that the three sets of double lines in the scanner mark can be read as the "Number of the Beast"—666. For them, this discovery amounts to the fulfillment of a further passage in Revelation which says, "... no one may buy or sell unless he has the mark, that is, the name of the beast or the number of its name." (Revelation 13:17)

But the champions of a worldwide conspiracy theory do not stop there—because the number "666" can be found lurking at many different points of global trade. In 1995, the Eurocard Company raffled off "666 exclusive perfumes;" in late 1999, a Swiss retail chain boasted of planting 666 "millennium trees." Various Internet and financial information centers use the number 666 in their reference numbers, etc. Anyone who searches for it obsessively can uncover evidence that the world is virtually infested with the "Number of the Beast"…

Some modern numerologists believe that they have identified the three double lines in a barcode as the "Number of the Beast."

Numerology and modern cash register scanners

Because the Revelation of St. John the Divine identifies evil and Satan's power in the world with the number "666," corresponding conspiracy theories flourish even today. The most recent numerological speculations about the number 666 claim that it can be found in product barcodes as well as in the Internet address abbreviation "www." Fantasists in numerical magic therefore explain that Internet addresses and the bar-code—which now appears on almost every product

The Revelation of St. John the Divine (the final book of the New Testament) speaks of the number 666; many modern Kabbalists consider it to be the symbol of evil itself.

MAGICAL ACTS AND CURSES

In ancient times, people wrote curses and maledictions on what were called curse tablets and secretly hid them somewhere close to the person for whom the curse was intended. Thus, for example, the Jewish prophet Jeremiah wrote all the misfortunes that he wished upon Babylon on a piece of parchment and ordered his servant, Seraiah, to carry the parchment to Babylon. Seraiah was then instructed to read the text out loud, tie the parchment to a stone, and throw it into the Euphrates River. The text on the parchment read: "Thus shall Babylon sink, and shall not rise." [Jeremiah 51:64]

In the practical Kabbalah, there are many formulas and actions that are intended to produce magical effects. The second-century text *Hekhalot Rabbati* ("The Greater Palaces") states that one can successfully gain "influence over others" by means of what the author called a central gaze, directed at the base of the other person's nose. The practitioner is then able to subject the other person's actions to his or her own will.

The demise of Babylon is thought to have been brought about by the prophet Jeremiah by means of magical acts.

MERKABAH MYSTICISM AND THE HALLS OF HEAVEN

One special form of Jewish Kabbalah is "Merkabah" mysticism; the name can be translated as "chariot of God." The Hebrew prophet Ezekiel describes his ecstatic vision of the throne-chariot of God ("merkabah"). What is known as the Kabbalistic Hekhalot literature recounts the experiences of a Kabbalist on his long journey through the seven palaces (Hebrew: "hekhalot") to the throne of God. Early practical Kabbalah maintained that anyone who studied this literature intensively would be able to approach God and utilize his power to influence life on earth. However, only a pure and initiated person would be allowed to step through the gates of the seven palaces, since the guards would require him to prove his knowledge of secret seals and passwords before granting him entry. But anyone who was indeed permitted—as Ezekiel was—to gaze upon the Divine seated on his throne would need to shield his or her eyes, because God is light and fire, and exceeds all human measurement.

The angel Metatron

Metatron is the angel who stands next to the throne of God and the second destination in the heavenly journey through the seven palaces. Kabbalists believe him to be the prophet Enoch, who, in his time, was assumed into heaven. He is permitted to sit beside the Most High for all time, and there he receives the Kabblists who, like him, have been able to successfully complete their journey. Practical Kabbalists therefore study the Book of Ezekiel (Chapter 1) and the Book of Enoch in minute detail, since there they can find direct instructions for the ascension of the soul to the throne of God.

The description of the "chariot of fire" in the Book of Ezekiel (Chapter 1) also captured the imagination of several modern authors. However, they see it less as a description of the journey of the prophet's soul, but rather as a detailed description of an extraterrestrial vehicle.

The Books of Enoch

The Books of Enoch are among the apocryphal literature (that is, they were not adopted into the canon of scripture). They were originally written in an Ethiopian, a Hebrew and a Slavonic version some time between the second century BC and third century AD. They contain revelations in which Enoch (Hebrew: "khanokh," the initiated one), the son of Cain, plays a central role. After living for 365 years, Enoch was assumed into heaven and was considered a "miracle of knowledge." The Ethiopian account describes the fall of the evil angels and the struggle between darkness and light. This version speaks of 200 fallen angels and their leader, Samyaza. These angels coupled with human women to conceive giant offspring, who fed on human beings. The people then turned to God to beg for help. The Hebrew version of the book describes the journey of Enoch's soul into heaven and his transformation into the angel Metatron.

THE SECRET OF GOD'S NAMES IN THE PRACTICAL KABBALAH

The Kabbalah considers the name of God to be an expression of his true nature. A person who knows God's name possesses the power inherent in him. This is the first rule of the practical Kabbalah, and it applies to the knowledge of all powerful names—also including the names of angels and demons. A further rule applies to the Hebrew language. Its alphabet expresses three different elements: an image, a number, and an idea. Each letter taken alone is a force that can cause something to happen. If several letters are combined in a certain context, this power is expanded—and all the more so if one attempts to determine the name of God. According to the Kabbalah, each of God's ten most important names releases a current of energy that travels through the universe as soon as it is recognized, read, written or spoken. It is this aspect, above all, which is emphasized in the modern Kabbalah, which aims to make itself available to everyone in the world (see p. 84).

A study of the Kabbalah requires intensive examination of the Hebrew language, to which it attributes immense power.

Kabbalah is also the study of the power of God's names and their invocation. Many years of practice and experience are required in order to perform these invocations correctly. Only then can the energy contained in them be set free and put to use.

The ten most important names of God

The names of God are used in amulets and invocations. They include the following: 1. AHYH—Ehieh/Eyeh (for some Kabbalists, the foundation and root of everything); 2. YA—Iah; 3. IEHOVAH—Iabe; 4. AL—El; 5. ALEIM—Elohim Gibor; 6. ELOE—Eloah; 7. YHWH SABAOTH—Tetragrammaton Sabaoth; 8. ALEIM SABAOTH—Elohim Sabaoht; 9. SDI—Sadai; 10. ADNI—Adonai Melekh.

The Invocation of Angels

In order to invoke an angel, one must first know its name. The 72 names of the angels can be found using the three mystical verses in the 14th chapter of the Book of Exodus, 14:19–21, which tell how God protected the Israelites during their flight out of Egypt by preceding them in the form of a pillar of fire, while an angel protected them from behind. When they reached the Red Sea, Moses parted the waters with his staff. Each one of these three verses consists of exactly 72 Hebrew letters. In order to determine the names of the angels, a Kabbalist first writes out the three verses in three lines—writing from right to left in Hebrew—and labels them with the numbers 19, 20, and 21, corresponding to the verses in the scripture. He or she then takes the first letter from verse 19, the last letter from verse 20, and again, the first letter from verse 21. These three letters identify the first angel. When one continues in the same way—that is, with the second letter of verse 19, the second-to-last from verse 20, and the second letter from verse 21, and so on—one can create a list of 72 descriptions or attributes of angels. These descriptions, however, are not yet their names. Up to this point, the Kabbalist only knows what the descriptions stand for—for example, "hope of all creatures" or "the one who imparts wisdom," etc.

An angel's complete name

Since all angels originated with God, they bear the attributes of the Most High within themselves because they embody his power. Therefore, Kabbalists attach one of two of the great names of God—"-el" or "-iah"—to each attribute. In this way, they formulate the 72 names of the angels or geniuses—or, as Yehuda Berg says, the 72 names of God. Angels are not God, but they represent him in each of their respective aspects. Thus, the first angel is called Vehuiah, the second Yeliel, the third Sitael, the ninth Heziel, the 20th Paheliah, the 36th Menadel ... and the 72nd Moumiah, who is responsible for health and long life.

In order to call upon an angel, a person must first determine its name using a quite complex procedure.

DREAMS: GOD SPEAKS TO HIS PEOPLE

Jacob dreamed of a ladder on which angels traveled up and down between earth and heaven. His son Joseph was sold to slave traders and taken to Egypt, where he was held in the pharaoh's prison. But because Joseph was especially gifted at interpreting dreams, the pharaoh had him brought to his court. Joseph interpreted the ruler's dreams and realized that the country was to experience seven years of abundant harvest followed by seven years of famine. Likewise, God appeared to the patriarch Abraham in his sleep when he wanted to speak with him.

Joseph interpreted the Pharaoh's dreams and recognized that seven years of rich harvest would be followed by seven years of famine.

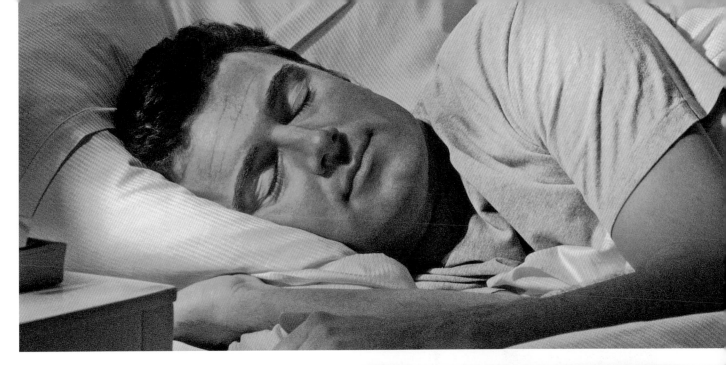

What happens to people when they sleep and dream? The Zohar says that the soul ascends aloft and experiences things it has never seen.

Nevertheless, the opinions of the rabbis toward dreams have not always been unanimous. While some saw them as messages from the Most High, others considered them to be illusions. Hasidim are convinced that all dreams express some sort of message from heaven, and in the Middle Ages it was a punishable offense to disturb a sleeping person on purpose. The Kabbalah considers dreams to be messages from God because the sleeping person becomes detached from his or her body and ascends into the higher realms.

The Zohar's position on dreams

The Zohar includes unequivocal statements on dreaming. During sleep the soul ascends aloft, and if it is worthy, it will witness things the dreamer has never seen. Nevertheless, the Zohar also says that bad people can be fooled by seemingly pleasant dreams and receive illusory messages about their future. When a bad person awakes and remembers a supposedly pleasant dream, he or she may be led to stray even further away from the right path.

The Kabbalah suggests that anyone who wishes to interpret dreams should call upon the Archangel Gabriel. Another option is to consult a rabbi or a good Kabbalist in order to avoid making a mistaken or self-centered interpretation of one's dreams.

Some Kabbalists advise people to call upon the Archangel Gabriel to interpret their dreams.

THE KABBALAH AND SEXUALITY

In contrast to Christianity, Judaism has always maintained a positive relationship to sexuality—particularly in the Kabbalah, which divides the universe into equally weighted feminine and masculine spheres, as illustrated by the Sefirot. In the view of the Kabbalah, at the time of Creation human beings were both female and male. It interprets the image of Eve receiving her life from Adam's rib as an intimate connection—a unity that emerged from within itself, just as God created the universe from within himself. The human sexual act is symbolically equated with God's actions in creating the world. Therefore, according to the Kabbalah, sexual pleasure is a means of coming closer to God. In addition, the lower Sefira "Yesod" represents the sexual act of conception, and since it is connected to all the other Sefirot sexuality is not seen as something separate, but rather on a level with rationality, emotion, and morality.

King Solomon and the Queen of Sheba

The Bible tells of the Queen of Sheba's visit to the court of King Solomon. After the host solved all the riddles this mysterious woman presented him, she made the following statement: "The LORD possessed me in the beginning of his way, before his works of old. I was set up from everlasting, from the beginning, or ever the earth was." (Proverbs 8:22–23). In the eyes of the Kabbalists, this self-assessment equates the Queen of Sheba with the second Sefira, that of wisdom (Chokhmah). King Solomon and the Queen of Sheba are thus understood to be a mystical couple whose mutual wisdom lies in the secrets of and the connection between the masculine and feminine. This connection is expressed in the Song of Solomon—an erotic text that describes the meeting of two lovers.

In the Bible, the Queen of Sheba says of herself, "I am beautiful." The emphasis, however, is not on her external beauty, but rather on her intellect—her wisdom and understanding.

THE KABBALAH IN THE CYCLE OF JEWISH HOLY DAYS

The traditional Jewish feast days are central to the ritual connection between God and his people. In addition, the cycle of holy days through the year symbolize historical milestones. A few feast days are particularly important to Kabbalists, who observe special rituals and endow them with further mystical levels of meaning.

Rosh Hashanah

The Jewish New Year is a time of reflection and inward contemplation. For Kabbalists, it also unifies the higher world with the earthly one: on this day, the two spheres are closer together than at any other time. To them, Rosh Hashanah represents the day of Creation, but also the time of God's judgment over his people.

Sukkoth, the Feast of Booths

Sukkoth commemorates the period of deprivation during the time that Moses led the Israelites through the desert. The faithful build grass huts (Hebrew: "sukkot") that resemble the shelters erected by the Israelites during this period in the desert, at the same symbolizing the transitory nature of all material possessions and the constancy of faith as well as its existence.

Passover (Pesach)

The Feast of Passover commemorates the Israelites' Exodus from Egypt. The feast symbolically reconstructs the situation of those people who, with God's help, made their way out of slavery in Egypt to the Promised Land. According to Kabbalists, the oppressed soul escapes the tyranny and constriction it has experienced here on earth. The name "Pesach" means "to spare" or "to pass over"; the holiday celebrates God's "passing over" of his people during the ten plagues he brought down upon Egypt.

Shavuot

On the fiftieth day after Passover Jews celebrate Shavuot, or the "Feast of Weeks." On Shavuot, the Torah—the divine instructions—was given to the Israelites, thereby sealing the covenant between God and human beings. Kabbalists think of Shavuot as a kind of "marriage celebration" between God and his people.

The Jewish liturgical calendar sets aside every seventh year as a "Sabbath year," in which the earth is allowed to regenerate itself and no farming is to be done. Here again, is the power of the number 7—for some simply symbolically; for followers of Kabbalism, in real terms.

THE CHRISTIAN KABBALAH

The Christian Kabbalah emerged in Europe around the end of the fifteenth century, when the fascination emanating from the Jewish Kabbalah reached Christian intellectual circles. Scholars such as Pico della Mirandola, Johannes Reuchlin, and Agrippa von Nettesheim sought a connection between the Kabbalah and Christian spirituality. Reuchlin, for example, noticed that the topmost section of the Sefirot—Kether, Chokhmah, and Binah—corresponded to the Christian Holy Trinity of Father, Son, and Holy Spirit. Pico della Mirandola, on the other hand, tried to use Kabbalistic methods to prove that the name "Jesus" was the full name of God. He compared the Hebrew word YHWH with the Hebrew word for Jesus—"Yehoshua," written JHSVH or YHSVH. Due to the fact that Yehoshua contained only one S more than the word for Yahweh, Mirandola concluded that Jesus must be the true son of God.

According to Johannes Reuchlin, the Christian Trinity (Father, Son, and Holy Spirit) corresponds to the three uppermost tiers of the Sefirot.

Kabbala Denudata

Another important exponent of Christian Kabbalah was Christian Knorr von Rosenroth (1636–1689). In 1677, he published his book *Kabbala Denudata* ("The Kabbalah Unveiled"), in which parts of the Zohar were translated into Latin for the first time. Knorr von Rosenroth pointed out that Jesus Christ is the Messiah who is prophesied in the Bible. To this day, his Kabbala Denudata is considered the standard text for the adaptation of ancient Hebrew mysticism, and it is the first text in which the term "Christian Kabbalah" appears.

Kabbalistic thought in Christianity

The Christian Kabbalists were particularly intrigued by the concept of the unfathomable beginning, Ein Sof, from which the Sefirot emanate. To them, God was Ein Sof and his son Jesus was Adam Kadmon, the mediator between the "urgrund" (the primordial source) and the world. According to Kabbalists of the Western world, Jesus contains the powers of the Sefirot, which in turn steer the powers of the urgrund through the universe. Spiritual creatures reside between God and human beings. In this concept—for the first time—the Jewish idea of angels is incorporated into Christian mysticism.

A Kabbalistic altarpiece

Since 1673, the Kabbalistic altarpiece of Princess Antonia von Württemberg (1613-1679) has been located in the Protestant church in Bad Teinach in Germany's Black Forest. The primary aim of this artistically gifted woman was acquainting the faithful of her time with the Christian understanding of salvation combined with Kabbalistic ideas. In the course of her own study of Hebrew, she encountered ancient Jewish mysticism. The motifs on the chart are primarily Biblical in origin. In creating it, the princess was less concerned with esotericism than with bringing the teaching of Christ into accord with the Kabbalah. A Swabian theologian, Friedrich Christopf Oetinger (1702–1782), went one step further. In the Book of Revelation, God is mentioned in a threefold phrase, namely "him which is, and which was, and which is to come" (Revelation 1:4), and seven spirits stand around his throne. To Oetinger, all of these things combine to reveal the ten Sefirot.

Johannes Reuchlin was fluent in Hebrew, and as a theologian he was convinced that the one God appears under many different names—for example, Allah. The greatest manifestation of God, Reuchlin said, is nevertheless Jesus Christ.

Pico della Mirandola is thought to be the first European philosopher to make an intensive study of Jewish mysticism. Were it not for his zealousness, the secrets of the Kabbalah probably would not have become known in the Western world until much later.

The *Kabbala Denudata*, published in the year 1677, contained the first Latin translation of parts of the Zohar. Even today, it is one of the standard texts used in the adaptation of Kabbalistic doctrine.

THE KABBALAH IN WESTERN ESOTERIC CIRCLES

Since the beginning of the last century, European oc-cultists and mystics have been fascinated by the Jewish Kabbalah. Eliphas Lévi (the pseudonym of Alphonse Louis Constant, 1810–1875) has already been men-tioned. In his book *Le Dogme et rituel de la Haute Magie* (1861; translated into English by Arthur Edward Waite as *Transcendental Magic, its Doctrine and Ritual*) he dealt extensively with Kabbalistic ideas and linked them to the 22 major arcana in the Tarot. In addition, parallel to the concept of the ten Sefirot, Lévi developed the idea of a negative counterpart—placing the "Klifah" in oppo-sition to the individual Sefirot. The process of confront-ing and overcoming these Klifah is a central theme of Lévi's "Kabbalah." "The devil is made from the tatters of God," he wrote; he was intrigued by the idea that even demons are nothing more than fallen angels, and that God consists of equal parts of light and shadow.

Aleister Crowley and the Kabbalah

Eliphas Lévi's theories were taken up by Aleister Crow-ley (1875–1947), perhaps the most famous occultist in the West. He encountered the Kabbalah early in life and was supremely impressed by it. Crowley defined magic as both a science and an art; in the mystical texts of the Kabbalah he sought to profoundly alter his own consciousness as well as to experience the superna-tural. Above all, he hoped to find descriptions of tech-niques for achieving astral projection (out-of-body experiences). Crowley associated astral projection with the soul's ability to detach itself from the body and—as the Ba'al Shem Tov once did—ascend into the world of the Sefirot. Here, the astral body is the psychic analog to the physical body—the vehicle in which Kabbalistic mystics can travel through the spiritual worlds.

The Order of the Golden Dawn

One secret society, which was founded in London in 1888 and to which many early twentieth-century

Aleister Crowley was anything but an unassuming and simple man. He saw himself as the incarnate Antichrist; some even thought he was Satan himself. He was fascinated by the Kabbalah throughout his life.

Like Aleister Crowley, the Irish writers Bram Stoker (left) and William Butler Yeats (right) were members of the secret society, the Order of the Golden Dawn.

writers and artists belonged—including Aleister Crowley and Irish authors William Butler Yeats (1865–1939) and Bram Stoker (1847–1912)—is the Order of the Golden Dawn. Its focus was the practice of magic.

The members of the secret society used incantations and rituals to invoke the positive Sefirot and their negative energies, the Klifahs, which the Adepts of the Order then fought against. In doing so, they called upon angels to provide them with strength. The better a person was able to do this, the more he or she could achieve in the Order.

There can be no immortality without initiation; immortality is achieved when a person's earthly nature unites itself with God—these are the axioms for the practical work of the Order, as essentially described by the occultist Israel Regardie (1907–1985) in 1937, when he broke his vow of secrecy. Until that time, he had been a member of what was probably the most mysterious hermetic society of the twentieth century.

Seven magical objects

Very much in the tradition of the Kabbalah, every person who was accepted into the Order of the Golden Dawn was required to make seven items with their own hands: a goblet for the element of water, a dagger for the air, a disk for the earth, a magic wand for fire, a sword for the fiery energy of Mars, a lotus wand for incantations, and a rose cross. Each of these insignia was assigned a particular color, as a connecting element between the spiritual and the material worlds. Color mysticism and Tarot cards were the basic magical tools used for various practices. Members of the Order used these things to invoke so-called astral visions, through which they attempted to advance deeply into the world of the unconscious.

The pentagram ritual of the Golden Dawn

One central ritual of the Order is based on the Sefirot: the pentagram ritual. In preparation for this rite, a room large enough for the master of ceremonies to make wide, sweeping movements with a ritual sword is lined with dark hangings and equipped with an altar, a gong, and candles. A magical circle, in which the ritual takes place, is drawn in the center of the room. As the circle is drawn the master says in Hebrew: "Touch your forehead and speak 'atah' [thou art], touch the middle of your solar plexus and speak 'Malkuth' [the kingdom], your right shoulder and speak 've-Gevurah' [and the power], the left shoulder and speak 've-Gedulah' [and the glory]. Clasp your hands together and speak 'le-olahm' [forever]." Christians will recognize the closing words of the Lord's Prayer. Complete concentration and inner calm are necessary for this ritual to be successful, as is precise observation of the prescribed procedure. "Then, facing East, trace a pentagram in the air, point the dagger sharply into its center and call out the name

YHWH—'Yahweh'; then trace a pentagram in the air facing South, call out 'Adonai'; then trace a pentagram to the West and call out 'Eh-yeh'; then a pentagram to the North, and call out 'Aglah'." This last word, Aglah, is an abbreviation for a Hebrew sentence—*Atah giborle-olahm adonai*—"Thou art ever powerful, o Lord," and was coined by the Order.

The pentagram ritual continues with the invocation of the four Archangels, and the member of the Order of the Golden Dawn concentrate deeply, imagining him or herself surrounded by flaming pentagrams.

The spiritual and the material

The Kabbalah teaches that the material kingdom, Malkuth—situated in the lowest, earthly realm of the Sefirot—is not separate from the spiritual world. Rather, the material is simply an illusion of the physical senses, which a Kabbalist can see through. There is no real opposition between the spiritual and the material. Buddhists have a similar view: they consider the material world an illusion.

Just as it did in magical rituals of the Middle Ages, the magic circle plays an important role in the pentagram ritual of the Order of the Golden Dawn.

1. Kether—the Supreme Being, his nature and his attributes
2. Chokhmah—cosmogony, the origin of the Universe
3. Binah—the Creation of the angels and of human beings
4. Chesed—the fate of people and angels
5. Gevurah—the nature of the soul
6. Tifereth—the nature of angels and demons
7. Netzach—the meaning and significance of love and sexuality
8. Hod—the significance of numbers
9. Yesod—the mysteries of the Hebrew alphabet
10. Malkuth—the balancing of opposites

Mathers translated the word Sefirot as "numbers, letters, and sounds" and interpreted the Creation as an act of divine magic. Mathers and his Order believed that by performing rituals and invoking the names of individual Sefirot, they could awaken their powers and make them accessible to human beings. The "how?" of this process was imparted to the members of the Order in the form of secret techniques.

The pentagram ritual of the Order of the Golden Dawn demands intense concentration, since visualization and precise imagination of the desired result play a central role.

The significance of the Tree of Life in esoteric Kabbalah

The founder of the Order of the Golden Dawn, MacGregor Mathers (1854–1918), wrote a number of books about the Kabbalah. In them, he reinterpreted the Sefirot and presented new ways of understanding them.

Even though Israel Regardie, a former member of the Order, broke his vow of silence after leaving the group, many aspects of the Order of the Golden Dawn's practices are still shrouded in mystery. As far as the pentagram ritual is concerned, we do know that it was carried out in a darkened room with candles, an altar, and a gong.

THE KABBALAH IN THE 20TH AND 21ST CENTURIES

In eighteenth and nineteenth century Europe, the Kabbalah had faded into obscurity. Even in traditional Jewish circles, although it was known about as a form of Jewish mysticism, it had virtually no influence on broader levels of the population. This situation changed in the early twentieth century. It was the Jewish religious historian Gershom Scholem (1897–1982) who, with his writings on the history of Jewish mysticism, Sabbatianism, and the Kabbalah, produced standard academic works on these subjects, thereby making the mystical traditions of Judaism accessible to modern Western thought. In the 1920s, Scholem taught at the Freies Jüdisches Lehrhaus ("Free Jewish House of Teaching") in Frankfurt, Germany; other instructors there included the psychoanalyst Erich Fromm and religious philosophers Martin Buber and Franz Rosenzweig.

Gershom Scholem

Gershom Scholem was raised in a traditional Jewish household in Berlin and planned to become a teacher in Prussia, first studying mathematics and physics. He then discovered the Kabbalah—and it never loosened its hold on him. His life's work made him the pioneer of scientific research into the ancient mystical sources of

Jewish religious historian Gershom Scholem had a decisive influence on the dissemination of the Kabbalah in the twentieth century. He made Jewish mysticism more accessible to modern Western thought.

The Kabbalah in the modern novel

In 1988, the Italian semiotician, art philosopher, and world-renowned author Umberto Eco (born 1932) published his novel *Foucault's Pendulum*, which deals with secret societies. In the novel, Abulafia is the name given to a computer that "guards" mysterious data by means of a protected password. Readers learn that the historical figure Abraham Abulafia (see p. 27) was the founder of a mystical science of combinations in which the four letters of God's name play a role—in what is called "chochmat ha-zeruf" combinatorial analysis.

Judaism. The starting point for his numerous studies were the same Kabbalistic books with which Pico della Mirandola began his research into the Kabbalah in 1486 (see p. 74), which led to the founding of the Christian Kabbalah movement. In his doctoral thesis, completed in 1920, Scholem wrote an extensive analysis of the book *Bahir*.

The Kabbalah, transmission of the Divine

For Scholem, the history of Judaism was revealed in the Kabbalah. Scholem himself approached the mystical traditions from a rational, academic standpoint—completely rejecting any esoteric concepts. Nevertheless, he was fascinated by the mystical texts, since they revealed the true character of the Jewish religion—namely, the expectation of salvation, that the Messiah would lead the people of Israel back to God's glory at the end of time. In one of his most important works, *On Kabbalah and its Symbolism*, he details his understanding of the doctrine and points out the original meaning of the word Kabbalah: "the transmission of the Divine." It is the power of the Divine that works through the Kabbalah. During his lifetime, Scholem fought against the esoteric reduction and transformation of the Kabbalah in circles such as the Golden Dawn, for whom it consisted of nothing more than mystical experiences. Instead, in his scientific works, Scholem demonstrates that like philosophy, the Kabbalah imparts knowledge about the world and the workings of God in the world.

In his books *The Name of the Rose* and *Foucault's Pendulum*, Italian author Umberto Eco deals ironically with such topics as medieval secret societies, black magic, and the Kabbalah.

The word "ecstasy," as used by the Kabbalist Abraham Abulafia and his modern descendent Moshe Idel, refers to a state of inner merging of the self with the Divine—regardless of the technique used to achieve this state.

The technique of ecstasy

Abraham Abulafia called his ecstatic technique the "Kabbalah of Names," stressing its distinction from the "Kabbalah of the Sefirot." The "ma'aseh merkavah"—the act of combining names—plays a central role in his technique. The Kabbalah of Names consists of mystical techniques for meditating on the names of God. In it, practitioners repeatedly pronounce, recite, and sing the individual names of God while performing specific breathing exercises and head movements, through which they aim to achieve an ecstatic state of abandonment and detachment from the self. In a further step, Abulafia transgressed the ban on speaking the divine name of YHWH. He attempted to deconstruct the holy name using every possible combination and vocalization of its letters. Using the interplay between practiced breathing techniques, special head movements, and monotone singing to reach the highest level of meditation, the practitioner aims to internalize the name of God.

Moshe Idel and Abraham Abulafia

The most important contemporary Kabbalist is the Israeli scholar Moshe Idel (b. 1947), a professor for Jewish Thought at Hebrew University in Jerusalem. Early in his career he began studying the work of Abraham Abulafia and discovered aspects of Abulafia's teachings that had previously been neglected. He calls this doctrine "the ecstatic Kabbalah" and describes it in detail in his book *The Mystical Experience in Abraham Abulafia.* In contrast to his teacher, Gershom Scholem, however, Idel definitely does place mystical aspects of the Kabbalah, such as techniques for approaching and uniting with the Divine, at the center of his observations.

Kabbalistic meditation according to Abulafia

According to Idel, anyone who wants to rediscover the Kabbalah today must devote him or herself to Kabbalistic meditation as it was taught by Abulafia. His techniques allow practitioners to achieve an ecstatic and prophetic state that approaches a mystical union with God. "The holy name of God," says Idel in his book, "contains more or less scientific interpretations of the cosmos and its workings, making it equally useful for its informative nature as well as for its magical power."

This form of the Kabbalah interprets the unique and absolute nature of God's name—through which God can be experienced—in a modern way. The almighty is present for the Kabbalist in the letters, a perspective which the scientific treatment of a scholar like Scholem did not allow for. Chochmat ha-zeruf, described by Umberto Eco in his novel *Foucault's Pendulum*, is the mystical science of combining the letters in the name of God. It provides insight into divine knowledge and makes it possible to directly experience the divine intellect. Abulafia's technique for achieving this type of experience of God is as follows: take a piece of parchment or paper, grab a quill and ink or a ballpoint pen—and write and combine the letters in God's name!

Union with God: "unio mystica"

The goal of the ecstatic Kabbalah—Abulafia's Kabbalah of Names—is a union with the divine intellect. Moshe Idel chose Abulafia as his role model, and according to his teachings, a person can take the first, intellectual step toward approaching God by writing and analyzing his name. This is called *devekuth*—"adhesion." In the second step, "adhesion" or "clinging" to the divine name evolves into a union with God's intellect, or *ichud*. This union is just like the state of "unio mystica" that is part of the Christian mystical tradition.

It sounds so simple when a Kabbalist says, "Take up your pen..." But like so many other aspects of Kabbalistic practice, the writing and combining of the Hebrew names of God as a first step toward union with the transcendental must be practiced over and over.

Yehuda Berg and the Kabbalah Centre

The most popular Kabbalist in the world today is Yehuda Berg. Pop icons such as Madonna consult with him, as do English soccer star David Beckham and film stars Elizabeth Taylor and Barbra Streisand. The increasingly widespread popularity of Kabbalah in recent years is in part thanks to his tireless activity throughout the world, and his propagation of ancient principles of Jewish mysticism. The Kabbalah Centres, which were founded by Berg's father, Philip "Rav" Berg, have become tremendously popular. Yehuda Berg sparked worldwide interest in *The Power of Kabbalah*, as his best-selling book is called. In it, he illustrates the significance of the Kabbalah in the life of every individual as well as for humanity as a whole. Kabbalah tells us that thoughts and ideas do not stem from the material matter of the brain at all. After all, says Berg, music does not originate inside a radio, either. Berg's deliberately informal style of communicating the wisdom of the Kabbalah wins over his audiences: he draws his readers directly out of their everyday lives, from current events in world politics, from their personal fears and hopes.

Who is Yehuda Berg?

Yehuda Berg's father, Philip Berg (born Feivel Gruberger) came to Israel from the United States as an insurance salesman in 1964. There he met Kabbalist Yehuda Brandwein, and a relationship developed that "changed the course of history," as visitors can read at the entrance to the Kabbalah Centre in Los Angeles. When Brandwein died in 1969, Philip Berg took up his torch and devoted himself to spreading his Kabbalistic message throughout the world. Berg and his wife Karen have founded more than forty Kabbalah Centres within the framework of the "Kabbalah Centre movement," thereby creating the world's largest organization exclusively devoted to the Kabbalah. The organization—now co-directed by Philip and Karen Berg's sons, Yehuda

Yehuda Berg, son of Kabbalah Centre founder Philip Berg, is on the path to great success. He has written a number of best-selling books about Kabbalah and established Kabbalah Centres in many major cities. His critics, however, maintain that he is overly focused on monetary gain.

and Michael Berg—also encompasses a Kabbalah Children's Academy as well as various Internet sites.

The Kabbalah as a formula for infinite power

In his books, *The Power of the Kabbalah* and *The 72 Names of God: Technology for the Soul*, Yehuda Berg identifies formulas through which we can radically change our lives and available opportunities. He draws upon a familiar example from the Bible: Moses parts the Red Sea so that the Israelites can cross without getting their feet wet and arrive safely on the other side. This passage in Exodus (14: 19–21) forms the foundation from which the 72 angels' names can be deduced. According to Berg, these are the 72 names of God, since angels are precisely the attributes of God himself. Berg is convinced that Moses used a special technique to overcome the laws of nature—namely, the formula of the 72 angels' names. Each of these names consists of three Hebrew letters. By means of these letter

sequences, the Unfathomable Light (God) is able to descend into the physical world. Berg also provides an example of the power that these divine names possess, since, according to Kabbalists, some of the names of God contain great healing powers.

A critical heart operation

Yehuda Berg tells of an acquaintance who needed to undergo a difficult heart operation. However, the surgeon could not operate because the patient's heart stopped beating repeatedly in the operating room, and a steady heartbeat could not be maintained. Berg selected a few of the 72 names of God to which special healing powers have been attributed. Outside the operating room, he prayed for the patient and meditated for just a few minutes on the chosen names of God—and was successful! These names, said Berg, contained the right "software" for his friend's body.

Yehuda Berg's books have become bestsellers throughout the world. They claim to help people transform their lives.

the right moment to put this Kabbalistic method to work. The areas of application for the 72 names range from "awakening healing powers" to "defense against negative energies" and "dissipation of the energy of death" (for example, in case of depression), to the "establishment of secure financial conditions."

Two examples

The following word stimulates healing powers:

מהש

It is composed of the same letters as the name "Moses." From time immemorial, Kabbalists have drawn spiritual strength from the names of the great leaders of the Israelites. Berg recommends that practitioners should imagine a blue light streaming through their bodies as they contemplate the letters.

The next word brings financial security:

סאל

Read from right to left it consists of the letters "Samekh" (that which supports), "Alef" (the essence of God), and "Lamed" (the learned one). These meanings convey the idea that happiness comes only from God.

Elizabeth Taylor (above) or famous Hollywood stars like Barbra Streisand (below)—who, in the film *Yentl* played a woman who dressed as a man in order to study the Torah, Talmud, and Kabbalah in the Jewish world—are enthusiastic followers of modern Kabbalah.

Fields of application for the 72 names of God

According to Yehuda Berg, the 72 names of God represent the "primary software" for the human body and its soul—and Berg intentionally uses computer terminology when talking about them. Anyone who contemplates these names, meditates on them, writes them down or speaks them aloud is "downloading" the names and their power into his or her own "operating system" at that moment. Even someone who is unfamiliar with the Hebrew language is advised to meditate intensively on the image of individual Hebrew letters. Berg understands "meditation" as the internalization of Hebrew formulas. The eyes scan each of the separate letters and save what they have seen on the "inner hard drive" of the brain. If you can then cover the image and visualize it in your mind, says Berg, you have reached

One of the most prominent devotees of the modern Kabbalah movement is pop singer Madonna. She has even written books for children that are based on the fundamental moral values of the Kabbalah.

The Kabbalah Centre movement

With 3.5 million followers worldwide, the Kabbalah Centre movement is headquartered in Los Angeles, California but has established more than fifty Centres in numerous cities around the world. Upon arriving at one of the Kabbalah Centres, visitors will immediately notice books like the Zohar located in the entryway and Hebrew letters on the walls. Learning the Kabbalah infuses a person with energy; he or she will need less sleep and live more harmoniously—so the Centres claim. When Michael Jackson was charged and finally acquitted of child molestation, he could be seen carrying a red string—the symbol of the new Kabbalah movement—during the trial. The string is said to release magical powers and protect the bearer against negative external energies.

Critical voices

The Kabbalah Centres established by the Berg family teach a new, modern conception of Jewish Kabbalah. They are open to all, Jewish or non-Jew, men and women, religious or secular. Yehuda Berg's stated goal is to reach as many people as possible in order to mobilize a "critical mass" that will inevitably bring about a positive transformation of the universe. But by no means all rabbis view these ideas favorably. Some see the movement as a type of "Jewish Scientology." Rumor has it, for example, that visitors to a Kabbalah Centre were asked to make five-figure contributions to the organization.

Nevertheless, in addition to the centres modeled in the style of Yehuda Berg, there are, of course other organizations that remain truer to the traditions of the Kabbalah—for example, the Bnei Baruch ("sons of Baruch") associations.

CLOSING WORDS

The Kabbalah fosters the health of both body and spirit and helps people to decipher secret personal messages and to keep their minds alert. But this is by no means everything: the Kabbalah has always been and remains an extremely varied and multi-faceted field of knowledge, which is equally fascinating to scholars in search of theological and philosophical insights as well as to practitioners of magic.

The primary intention of this book is to trace the major lines of tradition in this mystical Jewish doctrine and thereby make it accessible and approachable for a contemporary audience. By necessity, it was only possible to touch briefly upon certain topics, and others have not been included at all.

Anyone who is interested in the Kabbalah today can find a wide selection of information on the Internet. In addition, various Kabbalah schools are eager to court the favor of new adepts. The parallels and interconnections between the Kabbalah and the Tarot, Far Eastern doctrines of reincarnation, and Christian mysticism demonstrate that the mystical teachings of Judaism are part of an inexhaustible reservoir for spiritual seekers and knowledge-hungry pupils. Above and beyond any existing religious denominations, today the Kabbalah offers an alternative for the many people willing to devote themselves to the search for answers to existential questions including "Where did we come from?" and "Where are we going?"

The Kabbalah not only fosters health and knowledge, but it is also concerned with such existential questions as "Where did we come from?" and "Where are we going?"—questions that human beings have pondered since the very beginnings of time.

TIMETABLE OF THE EVOLUTION
OF THE KABBALAH

ca. 1900–1600 BC: Abraham lived in Mesopotamia and Canaan

ca. 1250 BC: Moses; the Exodus from Egypt

ca. 800 BC: The prophet Elijah

586 BC: Destruction of the first Temple in Jerusalem

586–538 BC: Babylonian captivity

ca. 520 BC: Construction of the second Temple in Jerusalem

ca. 200–300 BC: The Books of Enoch were written (Ethiopian, Hebrew, and Slavonic versions)

70 AD: Destruction of Jerusalem and the second Temple by the Romans

40–132 AD: Rabbi Akiva

2nd century: Simeon bar Yohai

ca. 200–1300: Hekhalot literature ("The Halls of Heaven")

ca. 500: Sefer Yetzirah ("Book of Formation/Creation"); completion of the Jerusalem Talmud

ca. 600: Completion of the Babylonian Talmud

ca. 1150: The Bahir ("Book of Brightness")

ca. 1160–1236: Isaac the Blind

1240–1291: Abraham Abulafia

1250–1305: Moses de León

1290: The Zohar

1463–1494: Pico della Mirandola (Founder of the Christian Kabbalah)

1455–1522: Johannes Reuchlin ("De arte cabbalistica")

1492: Expulsion of the Jews from Spain and Portugal

1522–1570: Moses Cordovero

1525–1609: Rabbi Judah Loew (Prague/golem)

1534–1572: Isaac Luria

1626–1676: Sabbatai Zewi

1636–1689: Christian Knorr von Rosenroth ("Kabbala Denudata")

1700–1760: Rabbi Israel ben Eliezer, called the Ba'al Shem Tov (Hasidism)

1884–1954: Rabbi Yehuda Ashlag, called the Baal Ha-Sulam

1887: Founding of the Order of the Golden Dawn in London

1897–1982: Gershom Scholem (the science of the Kabbalah)

1907–1991: Baruch Shalom Ashlag (Son of Rabbi Yehuda Ashlag)

1947: Birth of Moshe Idel

(Birth year unknown): Rabbi Yehuda Berg

GLOSSARY

Adam Kadmon—The primordial human according to the Kabbalah; also called the "celestial man"

Ba'al Shem Tov—The founder of Hasidism; also a symbolic name for a "master sage" who knows the name of God

Bahir—The Book of Brightness, which originated in the 12th century

Binah—The third Sefira: Intelligence

Chesed—The fourth Sefira, also called Gedulla: Mercy, love

Chochmat ha-zeruf—A method of combining the various names of God in order to achieve a state of ecstasy

Chokhmah—The second Sefira: Wisdom

Ein Sof—The "urgrund" or origin, the immaterial God of Creation

Elohim—A name of God (the Gods)

Emanation—The "outflow" of God's power from the "urgrund," Ein Sof

Gevurah—The fifth Sefira, also called Din: Power, judgment

Hasidism—A spiritual movement in Judaism that began in the 18th century

Hekhalot—Literature, texts concerning the "Halls of Heaven"

Hod—The eighth Sefira: Majesty

Kavanot—Aides to concentration in meditation or prayer

Kether—The first Sefira, also called Ayin ("nothingness"): the Crown

Klifah—The negative aspect of a Sefira (also totaling ten)

Malkuth—The tenth Sefira, also called Shekhinah: Kingdom, earth, ground

Metatron—The angel who stands next to God's throne

Mikvah—The Jewish ritual bath

Nephesh—Vegetative existence, one of the three parts of the human soul

Neshamah—Reason, one of the three parts of the human soul

Netzach—The seventh Sefira: Victory, eternity

Partzufim—Faces or aspects of the ten Sefirot (there are five masculine and five feminine)

Qlippoth—The shards of the vessels broken in the process of Creation, the cause of evil in the world

Ruach—Sensation, one of the three parts of the human soul

Sefer Yezirah—The Book of Formation/Creation

Sefirot—The powers of God which emanate from Ein Sof (singular: Sefira)

Talmud—Along with the Torah, the most important text in Judaism

Tifereth—The sixth Sefira: Compassion, beauty

Tikkun—Healing; perfection, reconstruction of the broken vessels (Qlippoth)

Torah—The Five Books of Moses (Pentateuch), contains the ethical and ritual laws of Judaism

Tzimtzum—Contraction; by contracting himself, God made room for Creation.

Yesod—The ninth Sefira: Basis, foundation

YHWH—The Tetragrammaton, the sacred name of God which is never spoken

Zohar—The most important book in the Kabbalah, probably originating in the 13th century

LITERATURE

Berg, Yehuda. *The 72 Names of God: Technology for the Soul*. New York, 2003.

Berg, Yehuda. *The Power of Kabbalah: Technology for the Soul*. New York, 2004.

Bischoff, Erich / Samuel Weiser, translators. *Kabbala: An Introduction to Jewish Mysticism and Its Secret Doctrine*. York Beach, ME, 1985.

Ginzberg, Louis. *The Legends of the Jews* (6 volumes). Boston, 1998.

Holroyd, Stuart. *Mysteries of the Inner Self* (Great Mysteries series). London, 1978.

Idel, Moshe. *The Mystical Experience in Abraham Abulafia*. New York, 1988.

Lampert, Vanessa. *Practical Kabbalah for Magic & Protection*. New York, 2002.

Lawrence, Shirley Blackwell. *The Secret Science of Numerology: The Hidden Meaning of Numbers and Letters*. Franklin Lakes, NJ, 2001.

Levi, Eliphas / A. E. Waite, translators. *Transcendental Magic*. York Beach, ME, 1972.

Matt, Daniel Chanan. *Zohar: Annotated & Explained*. Woodstock, VT, 2002.

Matt, Daniel C. *The Essential Kabbalah: The Heart of Jewish Mysticism*. San Francisco, 1996.

Munk, Michael L. *The Wisdom in the Hebrew Alphabet*. Brooklyn, NY, 1986.

Randel, Carla. *Farbe, Tarot und Kabbala*. Munich, 1994.

Regardie, Israel. *Foundations of Practical Magic*. New York, 1988.

Rosen, Jeremy. *Kabbalah Inspirations: Mystic Themes, Texts, and Symbols*. London, 2006.

Scholem, Gershom. *Origins of the Kabbalah*. Translated by Allan Arkush. Princeton, NJ, 1990.

———— *Das Buch Bahir*. Darmstadt, 1989.

———— *On the Kabbalah and Its Symbolism*. Translated by Ralph Manheim. New York, 1996.

Von Franz, Marie-Louise. *Number and Time: Reflections Leading Toward a Unification of Depth Psychology and Physics*. New York, 1986.

Wehr, Gerhard. *Kabbala*. Kreuzlingen/Munich, 2002.

Westcott, Wynn W. *Numbers—Their Occult Power and Mystic Virtues*. London, 1994.

www.kabbalah.com

PICTURE CREDITS

INDEX